SHAKESPEARE'S FREEDOM

The Rice University Campbell Lectures

Shakespeare's Freedom

STEPHEN GREENBLATT

THE UNIVERSITY OF CHICAGO PRESS :: CHICAGO AND LONDON

The University of Chicago Press, Chicago 60637
The University of Chicago Press, Ltd., London
© 2010 by The University of Chicago
All rights reserved. Published 2010
Printed in the United States of America

25 24 23 22 21 20 19 18 17 16   5 6 7 8 9

ISBN-13: 978-0-226-30666-7 (cloth)
ISBN-13: 978-0-226-30667-4 (paper)
ISBN-10: 0-226-30666-6 (cloth)
ISBN-10: 0-226-30667-4 (paper)

Library of Congress Cataloging-in-Publication Data
Greenblatt, Stephen, 1943–
    Shakespeare's freedom / Stephen Greeblatt.
        p. cm.
    Includes bibliographical references and index.
    ISBN-13: 978-0-226-30666-7 (cloth : alk. paper)
    ISBN-10: 0-226-30666-6 (cloth : alk. paper)
    1. Shakespeare, William, 1564–1616 — Criticism and interpretation.
    2. Shakespeare, William, 1564–1616 — Political and social views.
    3. Shakespeare, William, 1564–1616 — Philosophy. 4. Authority.
    5. Intellectual freedom. 6. Freedom of expression I. Title.
    PR2976.G738 2010
    822.3'3 — dc22   2010018917

To Charles Mee

Contents

Illustrations

Acknowledgments

At the beginning of *The Merchant of Venice*, the prodigal Bassanio is worrying about how he can, as he puts it, "get clear of all the debts I owe." If I have no comparable worry, it is only because I do not imagine for a minute that I can ever get clear of my debts and because I am grateful for having incurred them. Jeffrey Knapp read through the whole manuscript with characteristic wit, critical acumen, and generosity. I received many valuable suggestions from Timothy Bahti, Alan Dessen, and Paul Kottman, as well as from Alan Thomas, the editorial director for humanities at the University of Chicago Press, the copy editor Joel Score, and the Press's anonymous readers. For years now Homi Bhabha, Joseph Koerner, Thomas Laqueur, Robert Pinsky, and Moshe Safdie have been sustaining intellectual influences upon me, as well as cherished friends.

At the Institut für Sozialforschung at the Johann Wolfgang Goethe-Universität in Frankfurt, where three of these chapters had their genesis as the Adorno Lectures, I was hosted by Axel Honneth, whose introductions, questions, and comments were at once gracious and probing. Sidonia Blättler and Sandra Beaufays at the Institut, along with Klaus Reichert, Eva Gilmer, Carolin Meister, Roger Lüdeke, and Verena Lobsien, also helped to make my stay a richly memorable one. The Adorno Lectures were published by Suhrkamp Verlag, in a translation by Klaus Binder, as *Shakespeare: Freiheit, Schönheit, und die Grenzen des Hasses*. Two other German institutions deserve special mention. The first is the

Carl Friedrich von Siemens Stiftung in Munich, to whose director Heinrich Meier I am indebted for a very stimulating visit. The second is the Wissenschaftskolleg zu Berlin, which for almost fifteen years has been my intellectual second home. I am particularly indebted there to Horst Bredekamp, Reinhart Meyer-Kalkus, Luca Giuliani, Wolf Lepenies, and Raghavendra Gadagkar.

A revised version of the Adorno Lectures became the core of the Campbell Lectures at Rice University and hence the core of the current book. I am grateful for gracious hospitality to Dean Gary Wihl, along with Christine Medina, Robert Patten, and the members of the Rice English Department. It was especially pleasant to get to know Sarah Campbell and other members of the Campbell family, who had such a gratifyingly lively engagement in the occasion they had sponsored.

I have been fortunate to present pieces of this book as lectures on many other occasions, from every one of which I have received valuable suggestions, questions, and alternative perspectives. Among these occasions, I want to mention the Shakespeare Association of America annual meeting, held in Bermuda in 2005; the Una Lecture at the University of California, Berkeley; the Ropes Lecture at the University of Cincinnati; the Thatcher Lecture at Marin Academy; the Haley Lecture at Phillips Exeter Academy; the Stanley Fish Lecture at the University of Illinois at Chicago; the Meryl Norton Heart Lecture at the University of Northern Iowa; and the Jane Ruby Humanities Lecture at Wheaton College, as well as presentations at the University of Hawaii; the University of Utah; the University of Nevada, Las Vegas; the University of Science and Arts of Oklahoma; the University of Connecticut in Storrs; the Morgan Library; the University of Texas, Austin; the Dallas Museum of Art; the University of Wisconsin, Madison; Boston University; the Hathaway Brown School; Elizabethtown College; Davidson College; Austin College; Providence College; the University of Queens, Ontario; Emory University; Grand Valley State University; the New School; the Yale Legal Theory Workshop;

and my own university, Harvard. I was greatly honored as well to present some of this work as the Leslie Stephen Lecture at the University of Cambridge, the Royal Irish Academy Discourse in Dublin, and the Aptullah Kuran Memorial Lecture at Bogazici University in Istanbul, and at the Alfred Herrhausen Gesellschaft für Internationalen Dialog, Berlin; the Winfried Fluck Conference, Berlin; the Central European University, Budapest; the Nations Unlimited Festival, Stavanger, Norway; the Venice Center for International Jewish Studies; the Bibliotheca Alexandrina in Alexandria, Egypt; the University of Rome (Roma Tre); Pembroke College, Cambridge; the Spanish and Portuguese Society for English Renaissance Studies in Oporto, Portugal; the University of Warsaw; and the Institute for Doctoral Studies in the Visual Arts, Siena. I owe thanks to many people, both good friends and perfect strangers, at these and other institutions. A full listing would be very long indeed, but I would feel remiss were I not at least to acknowledge my gratitude to David Baker, Shaul Bassi, David Bevington, John Bowers, Dympna Callaghan, Richard and Rosalind Dearlove, Margreta de Grazia, Heather DuBrow, Edhem Eldem, John Feaver, Nilufer Gole, the late Gordon Hinckley, Christopher Hudgins, Bernhard Jussen, Louis Menand, Paul Morrison, Vincent Pecora, Istvan Rév, Ismail Seregeldin, Debora Shuger, James Simpson, Molly Easo Smith, Quentin Skinner, Teller, Nicholas Watson, Barry Weller, Charles Whitney, and Suzanne Wofford. I have received valuable research and manuscript assistance from Christine Barrett, Sol Kim Bentley, Rebecca Cook, Kelly Haigh, Beatrice Kitzinger, Emily Peterson, Joel Score, and Ben Woodring.

My deepest gratitude is to my three sons, Josh, Aaron, and Harry, and to my beloved wife Ramie Targoff. Ramie cannot be held responsible for anything that is amiss here, but, since we took pleasure together in talking through virtually everything in these pages, she should share the credit for whatever has any merit.

I am delighted to dedicate this book to a close friend and gifted playwright, Charles Mee.

CHAPTER ONE

Absolute Limits

Shakespeare as a writer is the embodiment of human freedom. He seems to have been able to fashion language to say anything he imagined, to conjure up any character, to express any emotion, to explore any idea. Though he lived his life as the bound subject of a monarch in a strictly hierarchical society that policed expression in speech and in print, he possessed what Hamlet calls a free soul. Free, a word that with its variants Shakespeare uses hundreds of times, means in his work the opposite of confined, imprisoned, subjected, constrained, and afraid to speak out. Those who are called free are unimpeded and untrammelled, generous and magnanimous, frank and open-minded. It is not only in hindsight that we recognize such qualities in Shakespeare. He was, said his friend and rival Ben Jonson, of a remarkably "open and free nature."[1]

Yet if Shakespeare is the epitome of freedom, he is also a figure of limits. These limits are not constraints on Shakespeare's imagination or literary genius. Doubtless there were such constraints—notwithstanding his aura of divinity, he was, after all, a mortal—but I am among those who are struck rather by the apparently unbounded power and visionary scope of his achievement. No, the limits that he embodied are ones he himself disclosed and explored throughout his career, whenever he directed his formidable intelligence to absolutes of any kind. These limits served as the enabling condition of his particular freedom.

Shakespeare lived in an absolutist world. More accurately,

he lived in a world pervaded by absolutist claims. These claims were not the relics of an earlier, cruder time; though they dressed themselves in the robes of antiquity, they represented something new. Religious radicals of Shakespeare's father's generation had successfully challenged the absolute authority of the Pope, only to erect comparably extreme claims for the authority of scripture and of faith. In the vision of English theologians inspired by Calvin, God was no longer a monarch with whom lowly mortals could negotiate by means of supplication, ascetic self-discipline, and other propitiatory offerings. Divine decisions were incomprehensible and irrevocable, unconstrained by any form of mediation, contract, or law. So too, crown lawyers for the two monarchs during whose reigns Shakespeare lived fashioned an elaborate conception of kingship above the law. Royal absolutism was a fiction—in reality, the will of the monarch was constrained by Parliament and by many other well-entrenched forces—and the absolute authority of scripture was comparably hedged about by innumerable limits. But the claims were made again and again, and, despite their obvious experiential failures, they did not seem simply absurd, echoing as they did the dominant vision of a universe governed by an absolute, omniscient, and omnipotent lord. Indeed, by Shakespeare's time the very idea of gods who possessed great but limited powers—the gods of the Greeks and the Romans—had come to seem incoherent, the consequence, it was thought, of putting demons in the place of the one true God.

With belief in an all-powerful God came an entwined set of linked absolutes: love, faith, grace, damnation, redemption. These conceptions had long since been stripped of any halfway or compromise postures in much Catholic theology and art: scenes of the Last Judgment on the portals of churches do not admit of unresolved cases or make room for a middle ground. The absolute nature of the core vision was, if anything, intensified by a Protestantism that rigorously eliminated Purgatory—the temporary middle-state of souls—swept away the mediating power of the saints and the Virgin Mary, and denied the efficacy of "works."

Shakespeare was not a theologian, and his work does not meddle in doctrinal claims, but he was raised in a culture whose official voices insisted on absolute divine freedom, unbounded divine love, faith alone, prevenient grace, eternal damnation, once-for-all salvation. And he heard, in the social and political theories that mirrored religious concepts, comparably extravagant claims for the authority of kings over their subjects, fathers over wives and children, the old over the young, the gentle over the base-born. What is striking is that his work, alert to every human fantasy and longing, is allergic to the absolutist strain so prevalent in his world, from the metaphysical to the mundane. His kings repeatedly discover the constraints within which they must function if they hope to survive. His generals draw lines on maps and issue peremptory commands, only to find that the reality on the ground defies their designs. So too his proud churchmen are mocked for pretensions, while religious visionaries, who claim to be in direct communication with the divine, are exposed as frauds.

Above all, perhaps, it is Shakespeare's lovers who encounter again and again the boundaries that society or nature sets to the most exalted and seemingly unconfined passions. "This is the monstruosity in love, lady," Troilus tells Cressida, "that the will is infinite and the execution confined; that the desire is boundless and the act a slave to limit" (*Troilus and Cressida* 3.2.75–77).[2] In a somewhat jauntier spirit, Rosalind assures the lovesick Orlando that "Men have died from time to time, and worms have eaten them, but not for love" (*As You Like It* 4.1.91–92). The peculiar magic of Shakespeare's comedies is that love's preciousness and intensity are not diminished by such exposure to limits but rather enhanced. And when lovers in the tragedies — Romeo and Juliet, Othello, Antony — refuse to acknowledge any limits, their refusal inevitably leads to death and destruction.[3]

My interest in this book is in the ways that Shakespeare establishes and explores the boundaries that hedge about the claims of the absolute. My focus in the chapters that follow is on four underlying concerns to which Shakespeare's imagination was drawn consistently and across the multiple genres in which he worked. These concerns are beauty—Shakespeare's growing doubts about the cult of featureless perfection and his interest in indelible marks; negation—his exploration of murderous hatred; authority—his simultaneous questioning and acceptance of the exercise of power, including his own; and autonomy—the status of artistic freedom in his work.

Though I intend the chapters to stand by themselves—each a distinct exploration of a critical node of interest in Shakespeare's work—they are linked to one another in an unfolding argument, bound up with the fact that my four principal concerns have all served as the objects of sustained theoretical reflection in the writing of Theodor Adorno. The philosopher was not in fact particularly interested in the English playwright and wrote very little about him, but many of the knotty aesthetic problems with which Adorno grappled throughout his career arose in the wake of what he called Shakespeare's "breakthrough into mortal and infinitely rich individuality."[4]

This breakthrough, I will argue, arose from an unexpected artistic swerve in his work, a startling departure from the norms of beauty that governed Renaissance taste. Shakespeare never formally repudiated these norms, but the figures who arouse the most fervent desire in his work—the Dark Lady of the sonnets, Venus, Cleopatra, and the succession of romantic heroines from Rosaline in *Love's Labour's Lost* to Innogen in *Cymbeline*—achieve individuation through their distance from conventional expectations. They are memorable, distinctive, and alluring not despite but precisely because of their failure to conform to the code of ideal featurelessness to which Shakespeare and his contemporaries subscribed. Departures from that code were understood to entail the risk of defect or stain, and indeed the forms of beauty in which Shakespeare seems most interested veer perilously close to what his culture characterized as ugliness. But that proximity is the price of individuation.

Radical individuation—the singularity of the person who fails or refuses to match the dominant cultural expectation and is thus marked as irremediably different—is suggestively present throughout the plays and poems but is perhaps most vividly exemplified not in Shakespeare's heroines but in two disturbing figures of otherness, Shylock and Othello. The Jew and the Moor do not merely run the risk of stain: they are what almost everyone in the dominant cultures in which they live defines as ugly. If Desdemona's love for Othello confirms the surprising proximity of supposed ugliness and beauty, the terms in which she articulates his allure reflect the continued power of the normative: "I saw Othello's visage in his mind" (1.3.251).

Otherness in *The Merchant of Venice* and *Othello* is far less a sign of allure than it is a magnet for hatred, a hatred that in the case of Shylock is not only directed at him but fully reciprocated by him and that virtually consumes the vicious Iago. To keep this hatred in check or to mold it to a socially viable end is one of the burdens of those in power. Such at least is the task of the duke and the law court in *Merchant* and of the senate in *Othello*. But the difficulty of the task—the ironies, constraints, mixed motives, and inadequacies that beset those in authority in both the comedy and the tragedy—is, as I try to show, part of a larger exploration in Shakespeare of the limits of power.

The only power that does not seem limited in Shakespeare's work is the artist's own. In the sphere of his sovereign genius the authority of the playwright and poet seems absolutely free and unconstrained. Nonetheless, Shakespeare, over the course of his career, repeatedly grappled with the question of whether he or anyone else could or should possess what we would call aesthetic autonomy. His most resonant response to the question, I suggest, is figured in Prospero's decision in *The Tempest* to break his staff and to plead for pardon:

As you from crimes would pardoned be,
Let your indulgence set me free. (Epilogue 19–20)

Prospero's words come at the very end of his play and near the
end of Shakespeare's own long, complex, twisting path though a
remarkably diverse body of poems and plays. At various points in
the course of this journey, driven by a compelling vision of individuality, Shakespeare finds beauty in the singular, confronts the
hatred aroused by otherness, explores the ethical perplexities
of power, and acknowledges limits to his own freedom. Though
they derive from the same vision, we should not expect these
recurrent strains in his work to occur all at once—they tend to
pull in different directions and to attach themselves to one or
another of the genres in which Shakespeare worked. But they
may be glimpsed all together for an instant, as if illuminated by
a sudden flash of lightning, within a single strange character.

There is a moment in *Measure for Measure,* Shakespeare's comedy of substitutes and substitutions, in which the disguised ruler
of Vienna, Duke Vincentio, needs a severed head, any head, to
trick his hypocritical deputy Angelo, who has ordered the execution of the good Claudio and has demanded that the victim's
head be brought to him personally. The death sentence is deeply
unfair but not illegal: Claudio is in technical violation of a statute
that makes fornication a capital crime. The fact that the statute
had never before been enforced, that Claudio and the pregnant
Juliet were married in all but the final, formal ceremony, and that
Angelo himself is conniving to commit fornication with Claudio's beautiful sister Isabella do not invalidate the conviction.

Pleading with Angelo for her brother's life, Isabella calls attention to the grotesque presumptuousness of those who exercise power over their fellow mortals. "Dressed in a little brief
authority," the petty officer storms about as if he were a god and

like an angry ape
Plays such fantastic tricks before high heaven

As makes the angels weep, who, with our spleens,
Would all themselves laugh mortal. (2.2.121–26)

When Angelo asks why she has directed these observations to
him, Isabella returns to the question of authority:

Because authority, though it err like others,
Hath yet a kind of medicine in itself
That skins the vice o'th'top. (2.2.137–39)[5]

But the ability of those in charge to conceal their own corrup-
tion—to produce a cover that hides the vice that lies beneath—is
beside the point. "The jury passing on the prisoner's life," Angelo has earlier remarked coolly, "May in the sworn twelve have
a thief or two / Guiltier than him they try" (2.1.19–21), but their
presence does not invalidate the law against thievery. So too the
law against fornication does not depend upon the uprightness of
the deputy who enforces it. "For my better satisfaction," orders
Angelo, conscious both of his own duplicity and of the legal va-
lidity of the sentence he is enforcing, "let me have Claudio's head
sent me by five" (4.2.113–14).

Though he is fully aware of the deputy's perfidy, the duke—
who has temporarily absented himself from rule and disguised
himself as a friar—cannot and will not simply declare the law to
be unjust. He connives instead to deceive Angelo with a piece of
legerdemain. It happens that another prisoner, a hardened murderer named Barnardine, is scheduled to be executed later that
same day, and the duke proposes that the prison provost simply
carry out the sentence a few hours early, so as to present Barnardine's head, instead of Claudio's, to the cruel Angelo.

The provost, whom Shakespeare represents as an unusual-
ly sympathetic human being, does not wince at the prospect of
shortening the convicted murderer's life. On the contrary, this
particular prisoner, as the provost describes him, seems to evoke
no sympathy at all from anyone in the play. In an odd, seemingly

gratuitous exchange—irrelevant to the complex plot of a play that is rapidly approaching its climax—Shakespeare provides a compressed sketch of a life worth losing. Each of the details is cunningly chosen to diminish sympathy:

DUKE What is that Barnardine, who is to be executed in th'afternoon?
PROVOST A Bohemian born, but here nursed up and bred; one that is a prisoner nine years old.
DUKE How came it that the absent Duke had not either delivered him to his liberty or executed him? I have heard it was ever his manner to do so.
PROVOST His friends still wrought reprieves for him; and indeed his fact, till now in the government of Lord Angelo, came not to an undoubtful proof.
DUKE It is now apparent?
PROVOST Most manifest, and not denied by himself. (4.2.119–29)

Barnardine is not a citizen of the city in which he lives and in which he has committed murder, but he does not have even the excuse of strangeness or unfamiliarity to mitigate his crime. Though conviction on a capital charge ordinarily brought immediate execution—punishments in Shakespeare's England were generally carried out directly after sentencing, as Claudio's was scheduled to be—Barnardine has been a prisoner for nine years, in part because of the contrivance of his friends and in part because of some uncertainty about his guilt. But now that guilt, "his fact," has been proven, and the criminal himself does not deny it.

Case closed. Even for a playwright with an effortless ability to conjure up vivid glimpses of lived lives, this amount of incidental detail might have seemed sufficient, but Shakespeare wanted more. If a nine-year imprisonment suggested that the murderer already had more time in the world than he deserved, it also raised the possibility of moral reformation, a subject to which the play repeatedly turns. Repentance would not ordinarily lead to a pardon—virtually all criminals were expected to repent before their sentences were carried out and to quail at the prospect of meeting their Maker—but it would slightly soften the picture and make the hastening of Barnardine's execution in order to provide a convenient severed head seem somewhat discordant.

The dialogue therefore goes on to close off that possibility:

DUKE Hath he borne himself penitently in prison? How seems he to be touched?

PROVOST A man that apprehends death no more dreadfully but as a drunken sleep; careless, reckless, and fearless of what's past, present, or to come; insensible of mortality, and desperately mortal.

DUKE He wants advice.

PROVOST He will hear none. He hath evermore had the liberty of the prison. Give him leave to escape hence, he would not. Drunk many times a day, if not many days entirely drunk. We have very often awaked him as if to carry him to execution, and showed him a seeming warrant for it; it hath not moved him at all. (4.2.130–41)

"Desperately mortal": the picture is of a man who is in effect morally dead, a man who neither seeks freedom nor fears extinction.

The fear of extinction had been given its most powerful articulation not in this play alone but in all of Shakespeare by the condemned Claudio, desperately pleading with his sister to help him escape his imminent execution:

Ay, but to die, and go we know not where;
To lie in cold obstruction, and to rot;
This sensible warm motion to become
A kneaded clod, and the dilated spirit
To bathe in fiery floods, or to reside
In thrilling region of thick-ribbèd ice;

To be imprisoned in the viewless winds,
And blown with restless violence round about
The pendent world; or to be worse than worst
Of those that lawless and incertain thought
Imagine howling—'tis too horrible!
The weariest and most loathèd worldly life
That age, ache, penury, and imprisonment
Can lay on nature is a paradise
To what we fear of death. (3.1.118–32)

It is in the context of this stupendous passage and of the fear of death that pervades the entire play that we encounter the strange Dostoevskian note sounded for a second or two before it vanishes: the kindly provost and his assistant have repeatedly awakened Barnardine, showed him a false warrant, and told him that he is about to be executed, only to find each time that the prisoner is completely unmoved.

Small wonder then that no one is concerned about shortening by a few hours the wretched Barnardine's wretched life. But to the idea of substituting one head for another, the provost does have an immediate practical objection: Angelo has seen both Claudio and Barnardine and will detect the trick. "O, death's a great disguiser," replies the disguised duke,

and you may add to it. Shave the head and tie the beard, and say it was the desire of the penitent to be so bared before his death; you know the course is common. (4.2.161–64)

One head will easily stand in for the other.

The provost has a second objection: he is an official, sworn to carry out the commands of his superior, and his superior has in this case explicitly ordered the execution of Claudio, with Barnardine's execution to follow only later that day. To this objection, the duke has a reply that also depends on the logic of interchangeability:

PROVOST Pardon me, good father, it is against my oath.
DUKE Were you sworn to the Duke or to the deputy?
PROVOST To him and to his substitutes. (4.2.167–69)

The scrupulous provost is then shown a letter that substitutes
for the substitute, a letter that stands for the duke's own will and
countermands Angelo's order. Of course, not just any letter will
do: the document must bear the signs that validate the substitution, here the handwriting and seal of the duke. The provost
is called upon to witness these signs: "You know the character,
I doubt not, and the signet is not strange to you" (4.2.177–78).

The sealed letter, substituting for the missing duke, displaces
the authority of the duke's substitute, his deputy Angelo, and li-
censes the plan to substitute one prisoner for another: "Call your
executioner, and off with Barnardine's head" (4.2.188–89). With
the help of a little human artifice—the head shaved, the beard
tied up—death will level or at least disguise all differences. Indeed, with the help of artifice, even among the living the differences are not very great. How else could the theater, which depends on a low-born actor convincingly miming a prince, thrive?
Echoing this root condition of the theater, the plot of *Measure
for Measure* turns on the venerable bed-trick, the familiar revelation that in the dark one lover's body is impossible to distinguish
from another. Substitution reigns.

In the immediate wake of the duke's command to behead
Barnardine, Shakespeare brings on the clown Pompey, promoted
from pimp to assistant executioner, to deliver a comical inventory of the other prisoners, many of whom he had come to know
as customers in the whorehouse:

First, here's young Master Rash. . . .Then is there here one Master Caper. . . .Then have we here young Dizzy, and young Master Deepvow, and Master Copperspur and Master Starve-lack-
ey the rapier and dagger man, and young Drophair that killed
lusty Pudding, and Master Forthright the tilter, and brave Mas-

ter Shoe-tie the great traveller, and wild Half-can that stabbed
Pots. (4.3.3–15)

The litany of fantastical names takes the audience back to characters in the morality plays of the mid-sixteenth century, characters with names like New Guise, Now-A-Days, Tipple, Desire,
Mischief, and Lusty Juventus. The names denote qualities or
conditions—indeed one of these plays is entitled *Common Conditions*—and they signal anonymity or, rather, an almost universal
fungibility. Anyone can become a Tipple or a Desire. Hence the
title of the greatest of the morality plays: *Everyman*.

But it is precisely at this point in *Measure for Measure* that something strange happens: in a surreal scene of utopian resistance,
Barnardine disrupts the logic of substitution by flatly refusing to
be executed. The chief executioner Abhorson and his assistant
Pompey call for the condemned man to "rise and be hanged":

ABHORSON   What ho, Barnardine!
BARNARDINE   [*within*] A pox o' your throats! Who makes that
   noise there? What are you?
POMPEY   Your friends, sir; the hangman. You must be so good, sir,
   to rise and be put to death.
BARNARDINE   Away, you rogue, away! I am sleepy.
ABHORSON   Tell him he must awake, and that quickly too.
POMPEY   Pray, Master Barnardine, awake till you are executed,
   and sleep afterwards.
ABHORSON   Go in to him and fetch him out.
POMPEY   He is coming, sir, he is coming. I hear his straw rustle.
   (4.3.18–30)

"I hear his straw rustle." The words, so perfect in their sim-
plicity, mark raw life, life in its most basic animal sense. And,
when he finally comes forth, this miserable drunken murderer
who has been penned up awaiting execution insists inexplicably

on his rights: "I will not consent to die this day, that's certain" (4.3.48–49). The insistence is absurd—the duke orders that he be dragged to the block. But the duke is a man of unusual moral sensitivity, and a moment later he has second thoughts:

A creature unprepared, unmeet for death;
And to transport him in the mind he is
Were damnable. (4.3.59–61)

The moral dilemma is quickly resolved: another prisoner, the duke is informed, has just died of a fever, and his head will do quite nicely. Barnardine is spared, and in the flurry of irrational pardons that closes the play, he too is released. There are no signs of penitence, no speeches of reformation. Only acquittal.

Whatever is going on here has little or nothing to do with realistic representation. We are in the realm of stage comedy, not of real life. London of the early seventeenth century was ringed with gibbets on which the bodies of criminals like Barnardine swung, and we can be sure that they were not given the opportunity to decline their execution. So what is going on? Barnardine is not necessary for the plot; the severed head comes, eventually, from someone else, the prisoner who conveniently succumbs to fever at just the right moment. He could just as well have succumbed earlier and spared us the peculiar spectacle of the unrepentant, intransigent, and inexplicably pardoned murderer. Barnardine, so unnecessary and so theatrically compelling, serves as an emblem of the freedom of the artist to remake the world.

But this strange character is—by Shakespeare's careful design—a most unlikely emblem of artistic freedom; penned up, drunken, filthy, and rustling in the straw, the convicted criminal Barnardine is the embodiment of everything that is mortal, bodily, and earth-bound. "Thou art said to have a stubborn soul," the duke says to him at the play's end,

That apprehends no further than this world,
And squar'st thy life according. Thou'rt condemned.
(5.1.474–76)

What follows immediately upon these words is the utterly implausible pardon, a pardon that serves as an emblem of the power of the sovereign over the life and death of his subjects and, still more, as an emblem of the playwright's power to suspend or alter all ordinary social rules. But, unlike the sovereign's, the playwright's power does not extend beyond the wooden walls of the playhouse. Many of Shakespeare's fellow playwrights — Christopher Marlowe, Thomas Kyd, Thomas Nashe, Ben Jonson, Thomas Middleton, and Thomas Dekker, among others — spent time in prison as a direct or indirect consequence of their writing. If Shakespeare managed to avoid this fate throughout his life, he understood very well that he too could easily find himself locked in a cell, rustling in the straw like the abject Barnardine.

Measure for Measure allows us to glimpse the seeds of what would in a later period be termed aesthetic autonomy, but the play is famously a "problem comedy," haunted by moral ambiguity, claustrophobia, and an overwhelming sense of something intractable in human nature. That it can be experienced as a comedy at all is bound up with yet another quality embodied in Barnardine: his intense, unexpected, and irreducible individuality.

Though he makes only a cameo appearance in the play, Barnardine is precisely not one of the faceless, interchangeable prisoners inventoried by the clown. His refusal to be used as a substitute is of a piece with his insistent peculiarity and particularity. It is as an individual that he makes his mark on the play — or better perhaps, given his moral and physical nature, his smudge. The diametrical opposite of an idealized or abstract character, Barnardine's identity is inseparable from what the duke calls the stubbornness of his soul, its refusal or inability to fit into a proper social norm.

The peculiar figure of Barnardine serves as a convenient introduction to two of the principal concerns of this book: first, the extent to which Shakespeare was able to conceive of his art as free to live by its own laws and, second, the extent to which Shakespeare fashioned individuality by departing from his culture's cherished norms. Shakespeare was fascinated by the dream of autonomy, a dream glimpsed both in Barnardine's peremptory refusal to consent to his hanging and in the duke's peremptory granting of Barnardine's pardon. There are, as we will see, much fuller and more elaborate explorations of these ideas in such plays as *A Midsummer Night's Dream* and *Coriolanus*. But both the conditions of the theater in which he worked and his own moral understanding led Shakespeare to hold back from extending the dream of autonomy to the artist himself.

Shakespeare understood his art to be dependent upon a social agreement, but he did not simply submit to the norms of his age. Rather, as I will argue, he at once embraced those norms and subverted them, finding an unexpected, paradoxical beauty in the smudges, marks, stains, scars, and wrinkles that had figured only as signs of ugliness and difference. Here too the irreducible individuality of Barnardine—at once ugly and oddly beautiful—serves as a convenient point of departure.

Barnardine, the unrepentant murderer whose first words are a curse, may serve as well as an introduction to another of this book's concerns: namely, Shakespeare's fascination with the way in which the dream of absolute freedom and the dream of absolute individuation fuse in intractable, murderous hatred. We know next to nothing about Barnardine's crime: only that he has killed someone and expressed no remorse for the act. But elsewhere in his work, Shakespeare explores in rich detail the relationship between negation and individuation. Thus—to take one of his greatest characters—it is through the desire to destroy that the haunting figure of Shylock marks emergence into individuality.

There are limits to Shylock's hatred: after all, he wishes to kill his enemy yet remain within the law. And there are limits to his individuation, or rather, the play's community contrives to compel him to convert and to vanish. Some years after *The Merchant of Venice* Shakespeare returned to the problem of hatred and imagined a figure for whom there were no limits and no vanishing. He gave his character the qualities of a demonic artist—a cunning playwright willing to stop at nothing in order to construct the perfect plot—and called him Iago. Iago's perverse refusal to speak at the close of *Othello* is the excruciating tragic equivalent of the comic silence with which Shakespeare ends Barnardine's story in *Measure for Measure*.

The strange pardon that Barnardine receives, in the midst of a scene of gratuitous, unmotivated pardons, directs us to yet another of this book's concerns: Shakespeare's deep sense of the ethical ambiguity of power, including his own theatrical power. The whole premise of *Measure for Measure* is the duke's uneasiness about ruling, an uneasiness that leads him to slip away from public view. He describes his secret withdrawal in strikingly antitheatrical terms:

> I love the people,
> But do not like to stage me to their eyes.
> Though it do well, I do not relish well
> Their loud applause and *aves* vehement;
> Nor do I think the man of safe discretion
> That does affect it. (1.1.67–72)

The duke subsequently reveals that he has a strategic motive for transferring authority to his deputy Angelo: for fourteen years he has failed to enforce the "strict statutes and most biting laws" (1.3.19) of his city, and in consequence respect for authority has virtually collapsed:

> Liberty plucks Justice by the nose,
> The baby beats the nurse, and quite athwart
> Goes all decorum. (1.3.29–31)

Were he suddenly to enforce the laws, after so many years of a "permissive pass" (1.3.38), he would be regarded as a tyrant, but his deputy "may in th'ambush of my name strike home" (1.3.41).

Such, in any case, is the duke's design, but it is a design that conspicuously fails. The deputy's enforcement of the laws is a disaster, and the duke can only resolve the tangle of hypocrisy, false accusations, slander, and arbitrary misuse of authority by staging the public, theatrical performance of himself, complete with loud applause and *aves* vehement, that he despised. His attempt to withdraw from power turns out to be impossible, and though his climactic display of manipulation, masking, unmasking, and pardoning spares the innocent—the play has a comic ending—he manages to leave the city in precisely the state of moral disorder with which it began.

The exercise of theatrical authority—authority in the state, authority on the stage—cannot easily be evaded. The duke's attempt at withdrawal, like comparable attempts elsewhere in Shakespeare's plays, has unexpected, potentially disastrous consequences. But Shakespeare does not unequivocally endorse what Claudio in *Measure for Measure* calls "the demigod Authority" (1.2.100). If to the guilty, publicly disgraced Angelo, the ruler, in his ability to perceive what is hidden, appears to be "like power divine" (5.1.361), to the irrepressible libertine Lucio he is "the old fantastical Duke of dark corners" (4.3.146–47). The play does not allow one to choose one or the other image or even to settle somewhere in between. Instead, as generations of audiences have attested, Shakespeare's "problem comedy" elicits a strange, uncomfortable response, a response conveyed in part by Adorno and Horkheimer's sour characterization of the culture industry: "There is laughter because there is nothing to laugh about." Or rather, as Isabella (herself a failed believer in absolutes) puts it, at the spectacle of human authority, in its glory and its thunderous absurdity, angels weep, but were they human, they would all die laughing.

CHAPTER TWO

Shakeſpearean Beauty Marks

Beauty, Leon Battista Alberti writes in an influential passage of the *Art of Building*, "is that reasoned harmony of all the parts within a body, so that nothing may be added, taken away, or altered, but for the worse." The cunning of this definition is its programmatic refusal of specificity. It is not this or that particular feature that makes something beautiful; rather it is an interrelation of all the parts in a whole. There is nothing superfluous and nothing wanting. As in Alberti's façade for Santa Maria Novella in Florence, which dates from the 1450s, the pleasure derives from the sense of symmetry, balance, and the elegant ratio of the constitutive elements (figure 1). Additions to this achieved whole, however attractive and eye-catching, constitute, in Alberti's view, not beauty but ornament. "Beauty is some inherent property, to be found suffused all through the body of that which may be called beautiful; whereas ornament, rather than being inherent, has the character of something attached or additional."[1]

This finely intelligent account, which works equally well for a building, a face, or a sonnet, helps to explain why there is so little specificity in Renaissance accounts of beauty, including Shakespeare's. Responses to beauty are everywhere in his work, and they are often remarkably intense, but for the most part they are, to borrow Musil's phrase, "without qualities." "Those parts of thee that the world's eye doth view," begins sonnet 69, "Want nothing that the thought of hearts can mend." The fact that

FIGURE 1. Leon Battista Alberti, façade of Santa Maria Novella, Florence
(built 1450). Photo: Erich Lessing/Art Resource, NY.

the young man's behavior gives rise to very different thoughts
about his inner life—"To thy fair flower add the rank smell of
weeds"—ironically frames but does not diminish the blank perfection of his outward form. The visible beauty of the beloved
literally leaves nothing to the imagination, and the fact that the

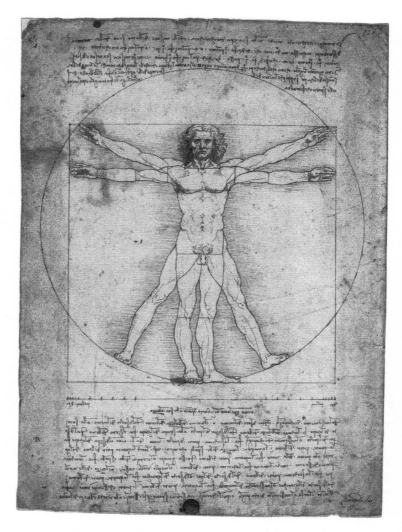

FIGURE 2. Leonardo da Vinci, *Vitruvian Man* (ca. 1485–90). Accademia, Venice. Photo: Scala/Art Resource, NY.

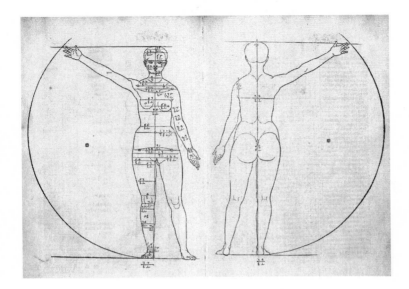

FIGURE 3. Albrecht Dürer, *Vier Bücher von Menschlicher Proportion* (1528). Houghton Library, Harvard University.

parts are not specified in any way only reinforces the sense that the effect is produced not by this or that attractive attribute but by a harmonious integration of ideal proportions (figures 2 and 3). Such integration was the dream of Renaissance artists, and we can glimpse its realization in a painting like Leonardo's *Lady with an Ermine* (plate 1), where the abstract lines of the schematic figures of perfection come to life, as it were, in the lines of the lady's clothing, jewelry, and hair. There is an extraordinary, highly individuated, and disturbing expressiveness in the painting, but it resides less in the lady's almost expressionless face than in her very strange hand and in the ermine that she holds. So too in Leonardo's portrait of Ginevra de' Benci, the spiky juniper trees in the background carry a peculiar, insistent intensity that the lady's flawless and psychologically inaccessible features conspicuously lack.

Those features, as literary and art historians have shown, were carefully calibrated in order to produce the overarching effect of harmony, a calibration that necessitated the suppression of any distinctive, individuating marks. The result was a virtually programmatic impersonality. In the wake of Petrarch and Boccaccio, Renaissance poets and painters established an ideal canon of beauty, with each constitutive part, from earlobes to feet, scrupulously diagrammed and cataloged. Of course, gifted artists understood that beauty could not mechanically be reproduced—the full effect would depend on such qualities as *vaghezza, leggiadria,* and *grazia.*[2] But the celebration of an elusive, inimitable lightness of being did not inhibit them from taking pleasure in the form known as the *blazon,* the descriptive enumeration of each of the parts that formed a perfect beauty.[3]

By the late sixteenth century this enumerative game was so familiar and shopworn that ambitious artists often marked their distance from it. Though he occasionally indulges in the blazon, Shakespeare is for the most part ironic about the rhetorical practice of the itemized list. Of course it made sense for a playwright—who anticipated that many different actors would play the parts he scripted—to leave out detailed physical description, even of an idealized kind, and the sonneteer had his own social motives for making it difficult to identify the beloved. But beyond professional tact here, there is a more general distaste for specificity in the praise of beauty. "Good Lord Boyet," declares the Princess in *Love's Labour's Lost,*

> my beauty, though but mean,
> Needs not the painted flourish of your praise.
> Beauty is bought by judgement of the eye,
> Not uttered by base sale of chapmen's tongues. (2.1.13–16)

The "judgement of the eye" takes in what Alberti calls the "reasoned harmony" of the whole, while the vulgar salesman cries up this or that particular feature. In the same spirit Olivia mocks Viola/Cesario's painstakingly memorized encomium:

> I will give out divers schedules of my beauty. It shall be inventoried and every particle and utensil labelled to my will, as, *item,* two lips, indifferent red; *item,* two grey eyes, with lids to them; *item,* one neck, one chin, and so forth.
> (*Twelfth Night* 1.5.214–18)

Viola immediately understands the social as well as aesthetic dimension of Olivia's mockery: "I see you what you are, you are too proud" (1.5.219).

But in this regard at least, Olivia is simply reflecting a broad-based consensus that too much detail in praise betrays a commercial intention. Biron begins to extol the virtue of his beloved's face—

> Of all complexions the culled sovereignty
> Do meet as at a fair in her fair cheek,
> Where several worthies make one dignity,
> Where nothing wants that want itself doth seek—

only to catch the marketplace implication of his own pun and to bring himself up short:

> Fie, painted rhetoric! O, she needs it not.
> To things of sale a seller's praise belongs. (*Love's Labour's Lost*
> 4.3.230–36)

It is precisely because he is not hawking goods at a fair that Biron, checking his impulse to enumerate the elements of Rosaline's beauty, forswears what he later calls the "maggot ostentation" (5.2.409).

Such ostentation is suitable for commodities offered in the

marketplace, a milieu Shakespeare—whose father sold gloves
from his shop—would have known extremely well. It is no accident that the best blazon in Shakespeare is of a horse:

> Round-hoofed, short-jointed, fetlocks shag and long,
> Broad breast, full eye, small head, and nostril wide,
> High crest, short ears, straight legs, and passing strong;
> Thin mane, thick tail, broad buttock, tender hide.
> (*Venus and Adonis* 295–98)

Human beauty cannot be so nakedly inventoried; it is simply
taken in by the enraptured eye. Indeed so little does the perception of beauty depend on individual features that the eye itself
may be shut: "Had I no eyes but ears, my ears would love / That
inward beauty and invisible," the lovesick Venus tells Adonis
(433–34). For Hamlet it is man himself, the paragon of animals,
that is "the beauty of the world" (2.2.296–97), while Iago bitterly
reflects that Cassio "hath a daily beauty in his life / That makes
me ugly" (5.1.19–20). These acknowledgments of the beautiful
are no less intense for being featureless.

Featurelessness is for Elizabethan culture the ideal form of
human beauty. In her many portraits the queen's clothes and jewels are depicted with fantastic attention to detail, but her face
again and again is a blank, expressionless mask (plate 2). Perhaps,
despite the intense emphasis on materiality in the representation of dress, the mask of the face is the Renaissance intimation
of what Schiller called the "annihilation of the material" in a truly
beautiful work of art or what Winckelmann termed the quality in
beauty of *Unbezeichnung*: "Beauty should be like the most perfect
water drawn from the lap of the spring, which, the less taste it
has, the healthier it is considered to be, because it is purified of
all foreign parts."[4] The figures Shakespeare celebrates as beautiful cannot altogether float free of matter, but the conspicuous
lack of content in the term *beauty*, as he uses it, is a gesture toward this freedom.

There are, to be sure, two qualities that Shakespeare does routinely identify with beauty. The first is radiance. Thus Suffolk is dazzled by the sight of Margaret in *1 Henry 6*:

As plays the sun upon the glassy stream,
Twinkling another counterfeited beam,
So seems this gorgeous beauty to mine eyes. (5.5.18–20)

And thus too Romeo likens the entombed Juliet to a lantern in the darkness:

For here lies Juliet, and her beauty makes
This vault a feasting presence full of light. (5.3.85–86)

Shakespeare often conveys the sense of beauty's radiance with the word "fair," which he uses more than seven hundred times in his work. "Fair" can denote lovely, clear, fine, or clean, but it also has the distinct sense of shining lightness. And this lightness of hair and whiteness of complexion in turn set off the pink of blushing cheeks and the deep red of beautiful lips.

The second recurrent quality of beauty is unblemished smoothness. "Hast thou beheld a fresher gentlewoman?" Petruchio asks, compelling Kate to greet the aged Vincentio as a "Fair lovely maid." And then, a moment later, he corrects the mistake: "This is a man, old, wrinkled, faded, withered" (*Taming of the Shrew* 4.6.30–44). Wrinkles repeatedly function in Shakespeare as the antithesis of the beautiful. The fair young man of the sonnets is urged to reproduce in order to secure his beauty from the ravages of time:

When forty winters shall besiege thy brow
And dig deep trenches in thy beauty's field,
Thy youth's proud livery, so gazed on now,
Will be a tattered weed, of small worth held.
(Sonnet 2)

These signs of age are hateful because they signify mortality:

> My glass shall not persuade me I am old
> So long as youth and thou are of one date;
> But when in thee time's furrows I behold,
> Then look I death my days should expiate.
> (Sonnet 22)

For at least some in Shakespeare's world, wrinkles signify more than age alone. The seventeenth-century astrologer Richard Saunders was drawing on an old physiognomic tradition when he composed his "metoposcopy," a guide to the interpretation of the lines in the face (and especially, as the term implies, the forehead). "He or she that hath such lines in the forehead," Saunders observes of one of his figures, "is mutable, unconstant, false, deceitfully treacherous, and of a vainglorious, proud mind" (figures 4 and 5). But wrinkles were feared and despised quite apart from what they prognosticated, for, in keeping with the dream of featurelessness, Shakespeare, like Winckelmann, repeatedly characterizes beauty as the *unmarked*.

Hostility in his plays therefore typically takes the form of a desire to leave marks. "Could I come near your beauty with my nails," the enraged Duchess of Gloucester sputters at Queen Margaret, "I'd set my ten commandments in your face" (2 *Henry 6* 1.3.145–46). To Richard's claim that her beauty has led him "To undertake the death of all the world, / So I might live one hour in your sweet bosom" (*Richard 3* 1.2.123–24), Lady Anne replies indignantly,

> If I thought that, I tell thee, homicide,
> These nails should rend that beauty from my cheeks.
> (*Richard 3* 1.2.125–26)

And Polixenes, enraged that his son has fallen in love with a peasant girl, threatens to mark her face:

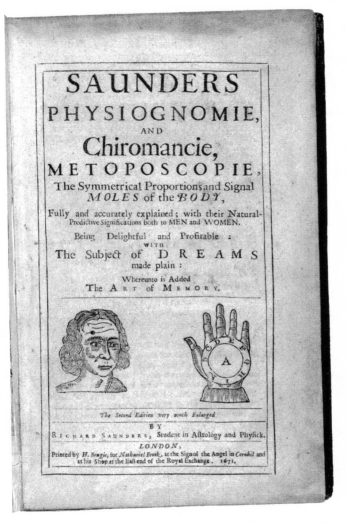

SAUNDERS

PHYSIOGNOMIE,

AND

Chiromancie,

METOPOSCOPIE,

The Symmetrical Proportions and Signal
MOLES of the *BODY*,

Fully and accurately explained ; with their Natural-
Predictive Significations both to MEN and WOMEN.

Being Delightful and Profitable :

WITH

The Subject of D R E A M S
made plain :

Whereunto is Added
The A R T of M E M O R Y.

The *Second Edition very much Enlarged*

B Y
R I C H A R D S A U N D E R S, Student in Astrology and Physick.

LONDON,
Printed by *H. Brugis*, for *Nathaniel Brook*, at the Sign of the Angel in *Cornhil* and
at his Shop at the East end of the Royal Exchange. 1671.

FIGURE 4. Richard Saunders, title page from *Physiognomie and Chiromancie* (1653). Houghton Library, Harvard University.

The lines of *Saturn* and *Mars* broken and difcontinued in this manner, fignifie hurt, and damage by falls.

He or fhe that hath fuch lines in the forehead, is mutable, unconftant, falfe, deceitfully treacherous, and of a vain glorious proud minde.

This

FIGURE 5. Richard Saunders, from *Physiognomie and Chiromancie* (1653). Houghton Library, Harvard University.

I'll have thy beauty scratched with briers and made
More homely than thy state. (*Winter's Tale* 4.4.413–14)

Scars, like wrinkles, are by definition ugly. There were in medieval and early modern Europe two significant cultural exceptions to this rule. The first were the scars on the bodies of martyrs and of Christ. These were the focus of lamentation, but they were also objects of intense religious meditation and aesthetic attention. In innumerable images from the period injuries are highlighted—as when Jesus is depicted calling attention to the gaping wound in his side or Catherine of Siena is shown kissing it. In some of these images the body itself entirely drops away, leaving only the wounds for pious viewers to dwell on with mingled pity, adoration, and something like erotic absorption (plate 3; figure 6). The idea of the beautiful wounds culminated in the stigmata of Francis of Assisi, but this cult was far too centrally identified with Catholicism to be translated comfortably into Protestant England. Shakespeare's characters often swear by God's wounds (at least until the censor forbade them to do so), but these wounds are the equivalent of expletives, not of adornment.

There was a second exception: on a soldier's body, scars are signs of honor. Thus Piero della Francesco's famous portrait of Federico da Montefeltro (figure 7), in profile, deliberately highlights the effect of the sword-chop on his nose. Shakespeare at least ambivalently endorses pride in such battle scars : "Show me one scar charactered on thy skin," York contemptuously tells Suffolk. "Men's flesh preserved so whole do seldom win" (2 *Henry 6* 3.1.300–301). "He that outlives this day," says Henry V to his troops on the eve of the Battle at Agincourt,

> Will yearly on the vigil feast his neighbours
> And say, 'Tomorrow is Saint Crispian.'
> Then will he strip his sleeve and show his scars
> And say, 'These wounds I had on Crispin's day.'
> (*Henry 5* 4.3.41, 45–48)

Volumnia even more enthusiastically celebrates the "large cicatrices" on her martial son's flesh (2.1.133–34). But only the ghastly mother of Coriolanus could characterize such scars as lovely:

> The breasts of Hecuba
> When she did suckle Hector looked not lovelier
> Than Hector's forehead when it spit forth blood.
> (*Coriolanus* 1.3.37–39)

Her aestheticizing and eroticizing of injury is precisely what is wrong with her. And there is certainly no equivalent idea anywhere in Shakespeare that scars on a woman could make her lovelier.

Even the one authentic woman warrior in Shakespeare's work, Joan la Pucelle, prides herself on her unblemished beauty. Though she had grown up as a shepherd's daughter, she tells the Dauphin, "And to sun's parching heat displayed my cheeks"

FIGURE 6. (Printed by) J. P. Steudner, *The Wounds of Christ, and a Nail* (late seventeenth century). Germanisches Nationalmuseum, Nuremberg.

FIGURE 7. Piero della Francesca, *Federico da Montefeltro* (ca. 1465). Uffizi, Florence. Photo: Scala/Art Resource, NY.

(*1 Henry 6* 1.3.56), she has been transformed by the apparition of
the Virgin:

> And whereas I was black and swart before,
> With those clear rays which she infused on me
> That beauty am I blest with, which you may see.
> (*1 Henry 6* 1.3.63–65)

So too, the soldier Othello, though he intends to take his wife's
life, cannot bear to mar her beautiful smoothness:

> Yet I'll not shed her blood,
> Nor scar that whiter skin of hers than snow,
> And smooth as monumental alabaster. (*Othello* 5.2.3–5)

There is, in Othello's murder of Desdemona, a perverse, per-
verted fantasy of undoing the hideous stain that he believes she
has brought upon herself and turning her again into the smooth,
unchanging paragon of beauty that he desires:

> Be thus when thou art dead, and I will kill thee
> And love thee after. (5.2.18–19)

This is the bitter end of the dream of a beauty impervious to time
and experience, invulnerable to the blemishes that age and injury
can bring. The thought of a scar on Desdemona's skin is worse
for Othello than the thought of Desdemona dead.

But ugliest of all in Shakespeare's world are the blemishes that
come not from age or injury but from birth. When Constance
in *King John* conjures up a catalog of disfigurements that make
one "Ugly and sland'rous to thy mother's womb," birthmarks are
prominent among them:

> Full of unpleasing blots and sightless stains,
> Lame, foolish, crooked, swart, prodigious,

Patched with foul moles and eye-offending marks.
(*King John* 2.2.44–47)

A prominent birthmark could be understood both as a personal misfortune and as a prodigy, an omen of public misfortunes to come. It could be seen as "sland'rous to thy mother's womb," because something the mother did or stared at or dreamed about during her pregnancy was likely to have caused it. The intense fear of this disgrace is why the blessings on the newlyweds at the close of *A Midsummer Night's Dream*—the couples have gone to bed and are imagined to be making love—focus so sharply on the threat of blemishes on the bodies of their offspring. "And the blots of nature's hand / Shall not in their issue stand," Oberon chants as fairies trip through the house:

Never mole, harelip, nor scar,
Nor mark prodigious such as are
Despisèd in nativity
Shall upon their children be.
(*Midsummer Night's Dream* 5.2.39–44)

All of this, of course, is entirely conventional, which is to say that it is part of the internalized cultural competence that governed the period's patterns of discrimination, response, and representation.[5] The thousands of Renaissance portraits and the acres of naked flesh that cover the walls of museums rarely depict birthmarks, though these must have been as plentiful then as they are now. The compulsion to erase the marks was extremely strong; perhaps it was one of the motives for wanting one's portrait painted in the first place. There are exceptions—as in, for example, a 1554 portrait of Mary Tudor (figure 8)—but these exceptions tend to signal a renunciation of the dream of perfect beauty and hence only to confirm its cultural hegemony.

    That dream marked a key difference between the portraiture of Rome, and especially of republican Rome, and Renais-

FIGURE 8. Anthonis Mor, *Queen Mary I* (1554). Museo del Prado, Madrid. Photo: Scala/Art Resource, NY. Note the mole (circled) on the right cheek.

sance portraiture. Renaissance artists, to be sure, were fascinated by the feats of aesthetic individuation evident in the portrait busts being unearthed from the classical past, and some fifteenth- and sixteenth-century sculptors brilliantly emulated these feats. Painters too, in Italy and still more in the North, produced astonishing representations of particular faces, indelibly marked by character, time, and experience. But when they aspired to represent the beautiful, Renaissance artists routinely erased all distinctive marks.

Among the many factors that contributed to the shift across the centuries, the principal one was the transforming power of Christianity. For centuries, Jesus and Mary were both routinely described, in the most literal as well as metaphoric sense, as immaculate, uniquely born without blemish or mark. Beauty, writes a mid-seventeenth-century English clergyman, "consists in three particulars; the perfection of the lineaments, the due proportion of them each to other, and the excellency and purity of the colour. They are all complete in the soul of Christ."[6] And it is not Christ's soul alone, the preacher observes, that is the epitome of perfect beauty, but his body as well. We think of children as possessing the sweetest beauty we are likely ever to encounter, but "even that beauty must needs have some kind of stain or mole, or some insensible kind of defect, though we know not what, nor how to term it, which was not in him."[7]

Such defect, in this time-honored Christian vision (a vision that effortlessly crossed the boundary dividing Catholic and Protestant), is the outward mark of the inner sin that stains all humans from their conception. Could we see with perfectly clear eyes, we would find nothing to praise in mortal bodies:

> Those cheeks that seem beauteous in their blushes, would be seen to have no other than the colour of our sins: those lips which we cry up for sweetness, would stink in our conceit with rottenness: the teeth that look white as Ivory, we should behold black with calumny and slander as the soot of the foulest Chimneys: the fair curlet locks, would look like snakes, the young spawn of the great red Dragon: the hands that look so white and delicate, would appear filthy, bloody, and unclean.[8]

That we are not disgusted by one another is merely the consequence of the congenital defect of our vision: "We, poor we, are but blind moles and bats." Were we not blind, we would see that Christ alone is truly beautiful. "No body but Christ's body."

Thus it is only in and with Christ, in the resurrected bodies of those who are saved, that human beings are cleansed of their unsightly blemishes. At the Last Judgment, according to theologians, all scars, wrinkles, and other marks on the flesh of the blessed would disappear, and each individual body would achieve its perfect form. All forms of "spottedness," as John Wilkins enumerated them—"Blemish, Blot, Blur, Mote, Mole, Freckle, Speck, Stain, Soil"—would be erased.[9] Everything that had been lost in the course of a lifetime would be fully restored—including, according the Aquinas, the enamel of the teeth. (The wounds of the holy martyrs, however, would, as a sign of honor, remain visible.)[10]

The dream that helps to shape Renaissance portraiture is this dream of the redeemed or resurrected face, cleansed of its mortal imperfections and depicted with surprising frequency (given the actual age-range of the sitters) as about thirty-three years old, the age of Jesus at his death. That age was often said to represent the height of his perfect beauty as a man—"the fairest of the Sons of men, through whose eyes, and face, and hands, and whole body, the rays of the Divine Beauty are continually darting from within"[11]—and hence the age at which all the saved, regardless of their actual age at death, would be resurrected. It is only with an awareness of this long history of erasure and longing for physical perfection that we can take in how unusual were the instructions that the Puritan Cromwell is said to have given to Sir Peter Lely: "My Lely, I desire you would use all your skill to paint my picture truly like me, and not flatter me at all, but remark all the roughness, pimples, warts and everything, otherwise I will never pay a farthing for it."[12] In his aesthetics as in his politics, Cromwell was toppling the existing order of things.

There was one important sphere in medieval and early modern Europe in which birthmarks and other unalterable distinguishing features on the body were routinely and carefully noted: the practice of identification. The historian Valentin Groebner, who has written a brilliant account of the signs of identity in this period, notes that special teams went through the killing fields in the wake of a battle and stripped the corpses of all clothes and weapons, in order to sell them. The dead in consequence were generally naked and difficult to identify, so that it was a challenge to determine which bodies should be honorably interred and which shoveled into hastily dug ditches. (One might recall a brief exchange at the beginning of *Much Ado about Nothing*. Leontes asks Don Pedro's messenger, "How many gentlemen have you lost in this action?" "But few of any sort," he replies, "and none of name" [1.1.5–6].) Relatives, intimate friends, pages, and the like would be called upon to identify the remains of those "of name." Thus in 1477 the naked and frozen corpse of Charles the Bold was found by his page who noted missing front teeth, a sore on his stomach, extremely long fingernails, and a tell-tale scar on his neck. Identity was established by signs in and on the body.

There were, apart from the warrior elite, several other categories of person in early modern Europe for whom unalterable distinguishing features were regarded as important and hence were carefully recorded for purposes of identification. Renaissance officials took a particular interest in those who were considered private property, akin to domesticated animals, and in those who were, in effect, the property of the state. Account books registered details—including complexion, hair color, and the form and location of any scars and moles—that marked the bodies of slaves. Similarly, "watchers," as they were called, lurked at ports or in alehouses or other public venues, armed with precise descriptions of suspected traitors and heretics. "The villain shall not 'scape," fumes Gloucester about his son Edgar;

> his picture
> I will send far and near, that all the kingdom
> May have due note of him. (*King Lear* 2.1.81–84)

Moreover, convicted criminals were routinely branded and mutilated, so that they would carry an indelible record of their offense for the rest of their lives.

None of this attention to the flesh contradicts what we have been saying about beauty: identity and beauty are in this period distinct, even opposed. The smooth, unblemished, radiantly fair, and essentially featureless face and body is the cultural ideal. This ideal is the ground bass against which Shakespeare surprisingly fashions so many of his remarkable creations.

But before we look more closely at these highly individuated and conspicuously unconventional characters, it is worth registering something anxious that haunts Shakespeare's visions of conventional, idealized beauty. "What find I here?" asks Bassanio, having chosen the right casket. "Fair Portia's counterfeit." There follows a very peculiar description:

> Here are severed lips
> Parted with sugar breath. So sweet a bar
> Should sunder such sweet friends. Here in her hairs
> The painter plays the spider, and hath woven
> A golden mesh t'untrap the hearts of men
> Faster than gnats in cobwebs. But her eyes—
> How could he see to do them? Having made one,
> Methinks it should have power to steal both his
> And leave itself unfurnished.
> (*Merchant of Venice* 3.2.114–15, 118–26)

This is, presumably, a moment of ecstasy, at once aesthetic and erotic, but the lines are charged with a sensation more like nausea: severed lips, hair like a spiderweb, a single eye eerily capable of stealing those of the beholder. If this is beauty, what is ugliness? What is going on here?

Perhaps Bassanio is expressing uneasiness not about beauty but about representation: he is, after all, contemplating Portia's picture and not Portia herself. (That fact is itself slightly odd theatrically, since Portia must stand and wait while Bassanio goes on and on about her image.) The ekphrasis focuses on the painter's uncanny power—"What demi-god/Hath come so near creation?" (3.2.115–16)—and on a quality of fear aroused by such power. Many years later, in *The Winter's Tale*, Shakespeare returned to the artist's eerie ability to rival great creating nature and staged an attempt to ward off the anxiety this ability provoked: "If this be magic, let it be an art/Lawful as eating" (5.3.110–11).

But in *The Merchant of Venice* it is not only the representation of beauty that is unnerving; beauty itself poses a problem. Bassanio articulates the problem in a speech just before he makes his fateful choice, a speech in which he persuades himself not to choose the obviously alluring gold and silver caskets, but instead to open the casket made of "meagre lead" (3.2.104). "Look on beauty," he says,

And you shall see 'tis purchased by the weight,
Which therein works a miracle in nature,
Making them lightest that wear most of it. (3.2.88–91)

The "miracle"—a violation of the rules of physics—is, of course, a joke: the heavier the makeup that produces the appearance of beauty, the lighter (that is, the more licentious) the woman.[13]

The misogynistic anxiety and disgust that surface here participate in a long tradition of traducing beauty. "Blinded by passion," observes Lucretius in a celebrated passage of *On the Nature of Things*, men attribute to women qualities that they do not actually possess.[14] Beauty in this account is the projection of desire; the moment at which the lover thinks he sees most clearly is precisely the moment of his complete blindness. To such a man, Lucretius mockingly writes, launching into a famous series of euphemisms, "a swarthy skin is 'honey–gold,' a slovenly slut 'beauty unadorned,' ... a wiry and woody wench 'a gazelle,' the dumpy and dwarfish 'one of the Graces, the quintessence of all charms,' while a huge hulking giantess is 'a sheer marvel, the embodiment of majesty.'"[15]

Shakespeare rehearses this mockery in *Two Gentlemen of Verona*, in an exchange between the lovesick Valentine, sighing over the fair Sylvia, and his servant Speed. "You never saw her since she was deformed," says Speed.

VALENTINE How long hath she been deformed?
SPEED Ever since you loved her.
VALENTINE I have loved her ever since I saw her, and still I see her beautiful.
SPEED If you love her you cannot see her.
VALENTINE Why?
SPEED Because love is blind. (2.1.56–63)

In ancient philosophy the way out of the blindness — the way to return to the state of calm indifference that protects a person from the vicissitudes and deformations of passion — is to grasp the extent to which beauty is, in Bassanio's words, "purchased by the weight." Even the most beautiful woman, writes Lucretius, makes liberal use of artificial enhancements: the poor wretch fumigates herself "with such foul perfumes that her maids give her a wide berth and giggle behind her back." Her lover meanwhile, his arms full of flowers, is standing outside on the threshold, planting "lovesick kisses on the door." But if, when the door is opened, he should get "just one whiff as he enters, he would seek a plausible pretext to take his leave . . . and then and there he would own himself a fool, on seeing that he had attributed to her more qualities than one ought to ascribe to a mortal."[16]

From this perspective, Bassanio, standing in front of the caskets, is trying to cool his ardent desire, so that he can see clearly and make the correct choice. The problem is that when he makes that choice and finds the picture of the lady, his rhetoric of praise is poisoned by the therapeutic course of irony through which he has just put himself, and his attempt to express ecstatic admiration comes out as queasiness.

There are many comparable moments elsewhere in Shakespeare, often linked to an obsession with cosmetics: "I have heard of your paintings," Hamlet tells Ophelia,

> God hath given you one face, and you make yourselves another. You jig, you amble, and you lisp, and nickname God's creatures, and make your wantonness your ignorance. Go to, I'll no more on't. It hath made me mad. (3.1.142–46)

But Hamlet's nauseated misogyny here is a symptom of his soul-sickness, not a sign of his philosophical wisdom. Anxiety about beauty is repeatedly voiced in Shakespeare, only to be repudiated. For Shakespeare at once acknowledges the compulsive, irrational, illusion-mongering power of desire—everything implied by the love-juice in *Midsummer Night's Dream*—and embraces it. Though the plays repeatedly explore the psychological force of projection, the audience is not, I think, invited to be ironic about the beauty of Portia, Juliet, Sylvia, or Ophelia. Instead the audience is invited to enter the state of illusion and submit to beauty's magic.

Shakespeare's great innovation is that the magic is, if anything, heightened when he turns, as he does again and again, to forms of beauty that violate the prevailing cultural norms: the witty Rosaline whose dark complexion leads Biron to assert that "No face is fair that is not full so black" (*Love's Labour's Lost* 4.3.249); the irresistibly seductive Egyptian queen who describes herself as one "with Phoebus' amorous pinches black, /And wrinkled deep in time" (*Antony and Cleopatra* 1.5.28–29); and, above all, the sonnets' radiant lady whose eyes are nothing like the sun (Sonnet 130). None of these figures is exactly a repudiation of the ideal type, for the celebration is always understood to be a paradox, a revelation of desire's ability to unsettle the proper order of things. But the beauty survives the paradox.

In a world in which the word "tan" has entirely negative connotations—time's accidents, laments sonnet 115, "Tan sacred

beauty"—the praise of darkness is an extravagant tribute to the
blinding power of the obsessed heart:

> In faith, I do not love thee with mine eyes,
> For they in thee a thousand errors note;
> But 'tis my heart that loves what they despise,
> Who in despite of view is pleased to dote. (Sonnet 141)

Here at least the eye is not deceived; elsewhere in the sonnets
to the dark lady, "sickly appetite" (Sonnet 147) undermines the
lover's ability rightly to see or to judge:

> O me, what eyes hath love put in my head,
> Which have no correspondence with true sight!
> Or if they have, where is my judgement fled,
> That censures falsely what they see aright? (Sonnet 148)

To censure falsely is to regard as beautiful what "true sight"
knows is ugly, and therefore to contradict the testimony of the
eyes or, as Shakespeare puts it in sonnet 152, to make "them swear
against the thing they see."

What this forswearing conjures up is a strange and momen-
tous shift in Shakespeare's representation not only of the beloved but also of his own voice. The poet speaks against his own
perceptions or against his judgment; he is a "perjured eye":

> For I have sworn thee fair—more perjured eye
> To swear against the truth so foul a lie. (Sonnet 152)

And this novel, compulsive, conflicted, and self-conscious speaking voice does what the speaker of the poems to the fair young
man never does: he identifies himself by name. He calls himself
"Will."[17]

Shakespeare's most intense celebrations of beauty repeatedly
violate the featurelessness that is his cultural ideal. And from

this violation comes an emergence into identity, distinct, peculiar, and unique, an emergence that characterizes not only the poet but also the dark lady and the other figures of paradoxical beauty in his works. Their description is not more detailed than that of the normative beauties—to be dark is no more singular than to be fair—but the departure from the norm itself acts out individuation.

With the dark lady of the sonnets or with Cleopatra, Shakespeare seems deliberately to be marking his distance from the aesthetic of completeness, the ideal form of beauty whose qualities Aquinas defined as *integritas, consonantia,* and *claritas* (and which Joyce's Stephen Dedalus translates as "wholeness, harmony, and radiance"). Instead of embodiments of just proportion, harmony, and symmetry, we have figures who are, in the perception of the age, "stained," and yet whose stain is part of their irresistible, disturbing appeal.

There was available to Shakespeare a conception of beauty notably different from the one, articulated by Alberti, with which we began. In such a conception brief touches of ugliness were cultivated in order to set off beauty all the more intensely. The practice of patching the face with pieces of black taffeta or very thin Spanish leather, cut into stars, crescents, and diamonds, began in the late sixteenth century (figure 9).[18] "Venus had her mole in her cheek, which made her more amiable," writes Lyly, ever alert to the newest fashion; "Helen her scar on her chin which Paris called *Cos amoris,* the whetstone of love."[19] Such "love-spots," as they came to be called in the seventeenth century, were meant to intensify the beauty of the circumambient flesh.[20]

Shakespeare very well understood this principle of highlighting and contrast. "These black masks," the sexually aroused Angelo tells Isabella,

Proclaim an enshield beauty ten times louder
Than beauty could, displayed. (*Measure for Measure* 2.4.79–81)

FIGURE 9. "Pedlar" (from *The Boursse of Reformation*, 1640) and "Patched Lady" (after a woodcut from Bulwer's *Anthropometamorphosis*, ca. 1650).

But Shakespeare's paradoxical dark beauties are something other than an attempt to render whiteness and smoothness more visible. Beauty inheres in the beloved's identity, including those aspects of the identity—strange, idiosyncratic, imperfect—that do not fit normative expectations. This is an erotics of wildness, contingency, and accident, not of organic perfection. And as such it makes a space, in the midst of the idealizing language of praise, for the conjunction of the art of love and the art of identification.

This conjunction is critically important, for it is far closer to the overarching aesthetic of Shakespeare's plays than the "reasoned harmony" and completeness of perfect form. About these plays it cannot be said that "nothing may be added, taken away, or altered, but for the worse." On the contrary, Shakespeare seems to have written with full awareness of the alterations, cuts, and additions that successful performance would inevitably entail. Virtually all of his plays spill out over conventional limits. Shakespeare seems to have delighted in this overflowing of the measure, this refusal to stay within fixed boundaries, just as he makes audiences delight in a succession of characters who do not conform to expectations comfortably embodied elsewhere in their worlds: Katherine rather than the fair Bianca, Beatrice rather than Hero, Rosalind rather than Celia, Cleopatra rather than Octavia. It is telling that when at the end of one of his most idiosyncratically structured plays, *The Winter's Tale*, Shakespeare represents the virtual resurrection of the beautiful Hermione, he goes out of his way to emphasize what Renaissance artists would have carefully effaced: "But yet, Paulina," the startled Leontes observes,

> Hermione was not so much wrinkled, nothing
> So agèd as this seems. (5.3.27–29)

What makes all of these heroines appealing—what makes them beautiful—is a quality of individuation that shatters the ideal of featurelessness.

The perfect emblem for this shattering in Shakespeare is the scene in *Cymbeline* in which the evil Giacomo closely observes the sleeping Innogen, so that he can persuade her husband Posthumus that he has seduced her. Initially Giacomo describes her body in ecstatic but entirely conventional terms, employing the formal blazon of which, as we have seen, Shakespeare was suspicious: complexion like "Fresh lily, /And whiter than the sheets!" (2.2.15–16); lips like "Rubies unparagoned" (2.2.17); eyelids "white and azure-laced/With blue of heaven's own tinct" (2.2.22–23). But then he notices what he calls a "voucher"—that is, a piece of evidence, suitable for a court of law:

> On her left breast
> A mole, cinque-spotted, like the crimson drops
> I'th' bottom of a cowslip. (2.2.37–39)

The mole is part of the story that Shakespeare adapted: the

heroine in Boccaccio has (in the English translation of 1620) "a small wart upon her left pap," while in the anonymous *Frederyke of Jennen* the sign is a "black wart" on her left arm. These stories in turn follow an old romance tradition epitomized in the thirteenth-century *Roman de la Violette*, which was repeatedly illustrated (figure 10). The illustrations, as may be seen from the sixteenth-century image reproduced here, carefully represent the tell-tale mole.

The sign on the flesh functions in Shakespeare's play, a play suffused with disguise and mistaking, as the indelible mark of identity, and not only for Innogen. Cymbeline recalls that his kidnapped son had

> Upon his neck a mole, a sanguine star.
> It was a mark of wonder. (5.6.365–66)

"This is he," Belarius replies,

> Who hath upon him still that natural stamp.
> It was wise nature's end in the donation
> To be his evidence now. (5.6.366–69)

Innogen's mole is likewise a "natural stamp," but the description—"cinque-spotted, like the crimson drops / I'th' bottom of a cowslip"—has a weird intensity of attention, poised between desire and revulsion, that seems in excess of its forensic function. "If you seek / For further satisfying," Giacomo tells Posthumus, at the climax of his vicious slander,

> under her breast—
> Worthy the pressing—lies a mole, right proud
> Of that most delicate lodging. By my life,
> I kissed it, and it gave me present hunger
> To feed again, though full. You do remember
> This stain upon her? (2.4.133–39)

Comment labiclle fift vng ptuit en la
paroit de la chambre affm que le côte.
de forest/vift lenfeigne que la belle Em̃
ant auoit fur fa devtre mamelle.

FIGURE 10. Anon., *Roman de la Violette ou de Gerard de Nevers* (fifteenth century). Note the mole (circled) on the right breast of the leftmost figure.

Posthumus remembers.

The mole on Innogen's breast, not Shakespeare's own invention but a plot device he characteristically lifted from someone else and then elaborated, is a seemingly decisive proof of sexual intimacy and hence of Innogen's infidelity. It is a stain, her devastated husband says, launching into the most violent expression of misogyny in all of Shakespeare, that confirms "Another stain as big as hell can hold" (2.4.140).[21] It functions then (like the spotted handkerchief in *Othello*) as a symbol of Innogen's genitals; a symbol more generally of the "woman's part" (2.5.20), the locus in Posthumus's misogynistic vision of all the sins that infect human life. But this vision is clearly revealed in *Cymbeline* to be a paranoid delusion, the consequence of a vicious slander. The slanderer, Giacomo, speaks of the mole as an erotic object—and nothing in the play repudiates this possibility—but it is a lie to regard it as an uncanny symbol of a moral stain, just as his claim to have kissed it is a lie. Instead, as its likeness to the delicate interior design of a beautiful flower suggests, Innogen's mole is something entirely natural and, as its use in the plot suggests, it is something at once innocent and individuating.

Innogen is beautiful, but she is not a featureless beauty. Her mole is not part of any formal perfection, but it is also not an ornament, either in the sense of an obvious adornment or in the sense of something merely added on and therefore dispensable. It is a mark of all that Shakespeare found indelibly beautiful in singularity and all that we identify as indelibly singular and beautiful in his work.

{ CHAPTER THREE }

The Limits of Hatred

Here is the situation. There is on the body politic an unsightly stain, an excrescence from which we instinctively avert our eyes. But pretending that we do not see the disfigurement is as dangerous as ignoring a strange mole growing on the skin. For we have, living in our midst, an alien population who hate us, as the saying goes, with a vengeance. To hate us with a vengeance means that, despite the fact that we tolerate their presence and allow them the benefits of our civic order (benefits they have enjoyed for generations), these aliens feel that they have been injured by us, and this feeling of injury justifies in their twisted minds any hostile measures that they might choose to take. Since we are fully at home here and are stronger than they are—we embody the dominant values, embrace the dominant beliefs, control the dominant institutions—the hostile measures to which their hatred drives them will almost invariably be sly and covert. When they see us, they bow obsequiously, as if they were courting our friendship, but the pretence is almost comically unconvincing.

For the most part they keep to themselves and associate only with one another. Who else would put up with them? Of course they cannot keep entirely apart: they buy from us and sell to us, and in doing so they must talk with us and walk with us. But participation in the economic life of our city, observing its regulations and protected by its laws, has created in them no loyalty. On the contrary, their hatred only builds, and it is met, I freely grant, by a reciprocal loathing, when we deign even to give them a thought. It is difficult sometimes to think of these aliens as fully human, so much are they like vicious dogs, kept in check only through the kicks and curses that serve to remind them who is in charge. For like vicious dogs, when given the chance, they will bite.

But after all, they are not mere animals. Indeed, though they are constantly reminded of our contempt for them, they regard themselves as in some ineffable way our superiors. Filth as they are and cloaked with a show of humility, they imagine themselves radiant in the possession of the sole truth, a truth embodied in a book that they embrace with fanatical devotion. The book inflames their vindictive hatred of anyone who lies outside the charmed circle of the faithful. They pore over the ancient stories with an exegetical cunning that enables them to license behavior toward nonbelievers that any decent person would immediately understand to be immoral. And this cunning has made them adept in manipulating to their advantage our institutions and practices. They understand that we believe in the rule of law, just as we believe in the market. Hence they sign contracts with us and run to court if the precise terms of these contracts are not punctiliously observed. As they are sly and we often trusting and innocent, they frequently get the better of us.

But it is as if profiting from their interactions with us—and make no mistake, they profit mightily, so that their houses are crammed with hidden gold and jewels—only exacerbates their hatred. They would never dream of doing with us what we routinely do with one another: taking things on trust, sealing agreements with a simple handshake, sitting down together in a spirit of generosity and kindness. Why, they refuse to eat or drink with us—the most basic signs of human fellowship. What does it mean, when we have overcome our natural revulsion and invited them to join us for a meal, that they decline our invitation? It means that they regard our very food as unclean and that, preferring to remain alien, they hold themselves apart. That is why they will not participate in or even watch our festivities, celebrated everywhere in the world and treasured by everyone but them. When we parade by their houses, they lock the doors and shutter the windows, trying to keep even the sound of our joyous music from reaching the ears of those inside.

They are particularly frantic, of course, about a certain group of those shut away inside their houses, namely their women— above all, their precious daughters, some of whom are surprisingly beautiful. (Beauty often springs from the most implausible soil.) It is not so much that the fathers love their daughters as that they fear losing them, as they put it, to us. "Losing them"— as if escape from suffocating enclosure were a loss. The women in these households are little better than slaves. Small wonder that they dream of running away with our young men and living the unconstrained lives of our women. These dreams send the alien parents into a panic. They would rather see their daughters dead at their feet, the fathers declare, than have them behave the way our women do, with a boldness and liberty that they attribute only to prostitutes.

What is it about modernity that they hate so? Are they threatened by our freedom, or is it the feeling that they have been excluded from it that enrages them? If the latter is the case, do they attribute their exclusion entirely to our ill will or is their resentment sharpened by a gnawing consciousness of their own inadequacy? They are, after all, the embodiments of a great historical failure. No matter how well off one or another of them may be, no matter how impressive their past cultural glories, the fact is that they have been superseded. They are history's castoffs, and there is no way in which they can catch up.

Their only hope is to become like us, the way so many groups, in the wake of comparable cultural failures, have done. And, because we are strong by nature and because our culture is generous and embracing, we would welcome them and make them feel truly at home. Well, perhaps not immediately, perhaps not in the first generation. But quickly enough their children and their children's children would lose the musty smell of isolation and become indistinguishable from us. They would be full, free citizens. Only their names might betray their alien origins, and after all there is nothing easier to change than a name.

Instead they cling stubbornly, these aliens among us, to beliefs that are hopelessly outdated, and of course they cling to their seething hatred. Among themselves they no doubt share their resentment of us and nurse their sense of injury. Hatred is like a drug to which they are addicted; it poisons them, but they cannot live without it. Whenever two of them meet, they voice their litany of complaints and loathing—as if each of them had suffered more than anyone in the world—and they plot revenge. Their hatred is stirred to a boil in the place that they claim is a house of worship: not a refuge of mercy but a breeding ground of chicanery, fanaticism, and murderousness. It is late in the day. Long before this we should have listened to those who were warning us about our enemies. We may awaken one day and find ourselves enmeshed in a plot aimed at innocent lives. Such a plot may use as a weapon the very system that brings us together with the aliens in a shared civic life. And if this terrible day comes, we will have to figure out how to save our own without jettisoning our rule of law, for it is that rule of law that gives our culture its ability to prosper. But what, I wonder, is the legal remedy against hatred?

Now, more than ever, *The Merchant of Venice* has a weird, uneasy relevance, a sense at once fascinating and disagreeable that it is playing with fire. All my life I thought of the combustible material as anti-Semitism—or, to put it more carefully, Christianity's Jewish problem. "Go, Tubal, and meet me at our synagogue. Go, good Tubal; at our synagogue, Tubal" (3.1.107–8). But the queasiness of Western cities no longer centers on the synagogue. It takes, as I hope I have shown, only a small adjustment to tap into current fears: "Go, Tubal, and meet me at our mosque. Go, good Tubal; at our mosque, Tubal."

What is the meaning of the adjustment, or rather of the ease with which the adjustment can be made? The answer might conceivably be found in the theory, articulated most influentially in our own time by Carl Schmitt but reaching back at least to Hobbes, that the political, the sphere of the state, is constituted by the distinction between friends and enemies: "Every religious, moral, economic, ethical, or other antithesis," writes Schmitt, "transforms into a political one if it is sufficiently strong to group human beings effectively according to friend and enemy."[1] The theory claims that this constitutive distinction is effectively without content. It is not, of course, without content for the particular parties identified at any one time and in any one place as enemies; they all too readily fill in the blanks created by the structural opposition with a host of highly specific charges. But these charges turn out to be accidents, in the Aristotelian sense of the term; the substance is the oppositional structure itself, a structure into which virtually any particulars can be inserted in what amounts to a process of pure—that is, contentless—cultural mobility.

But is the mobility here actually devoid of content? We are not, after all, speaking of some random substitution. It can hardly be an accident that the two principal historical enemies of Christianity, Judaism and Islam, succeed each other so easily in the imaginative structure created by Shakespeare's comedy of friendship and enmity. They were already linked in the vision of enmity and in the representation and expression of hatred: as in Bosch's paintings of the tormenters of Christ, where the signs of Islam mingle with those of Judaism (plate 4), or in the Croxton Play of the Sacrament, where the villainous Jews swear by Mohammed. In the great courtroom scene *The Merchant of Venice* stages an appeal to mercy as a universal human value that transcends all local enmities, all sectarian differences, all political and legal systems that attempt to compel—Shakespeare's word is "strain"—their desired results:

> The quality of mercy is not strained.
> It droppeth as the gentle rain from heaven
> Upon the place beneath. (4.1.179–81)

But Shakespeare is cunningly careful to bring this appeal to a distinctly doctrinal climax:

> Therefore, Jew,
> Though justice be thy plea, consider this:
> That in the course of justice none of us
> Should see salvation. We do pray for mercy,
> And that same prayer doth teach us all to render
> The deeds of mercy. (4.1.192–97)

Portia's invocation of the Lord's Prayer and the hope of salvation anticipates the final solution to the dilemma of hatred that the play will shortly reach: the forced conversion of Shylock to Christianity.

"Forced" is perhaps not quite right. Compulsion is an unwelcome guest at comedy's banquet. Christianity linked its eschatological hopes to the conversion of the Jews, but it did not want its generous offer of salvation to be tainted by the execution of those who refused to be saved. Jews could be made to feel the consequences of their stubbornness — spat upon, beaten, forced to live in ghettos, excluded from most occupations, wantonly robbed, and on occasion abandoned to the homicidal wrath of the mob — but they could not simply be told that they must convert or die. Hence in Shakespeare's Venetian courtroom, Shylock's "consent" is specifically solicited:

PORTIA Art thou contented, Jew? What dost thou say?
SHYLOCK I am content. (4.1.388–89)

But, of course, the Duke has just declared explicitly that Shylock "shall do this, or else I do recant / The pardon that I late pronouncèd here" (4.1.386–87). The pardon in question is of a death sentence. So the guilty Jew is given the choice of losing his life or converting. He chooses, perhaps not surprisingly, to become a Christian and thereby to ratify his own absorption and that of his only child into the dominant religion and the dominant culture. And with that absorption, he disappears:

> I pray you give me leave to go from hence.
> I am not well. (4.1.391–92)

Shylock's disappearance marks the end of the powerful, dangerous negation that structures the first four acts of *The Merchant of Venice*, and it serves too as a convenient emblem of the eventual disappearance of the "Jewish Question" from the agenda of most European nations. It is this disappearance—facilitated by an orgy of mass murder, by intermarriage and religious conversion, and by assimilation and citizenship[2]—that has created a vacant space, as I have proposed, for the convenient substitution of Christianity's other great enemy, Islam.

But the ease of this substitution masks significant differences between the enemies, differences that will enable us to illuminate particular aspects of Shylock's character and the play's solution to his hatred. The anxiety currently provoked by a militant, murderous strain of fundamentalist Islam may be fanned by a sensationalist press and exploited by unscrupulous politicians, but it is attached to real and quite terrible events. The actual relationship of these events to particular currents in a major world religion is a matter for serious study and ongoing debate—scholars have observed that even tactics, such as suicide bombing, that are explicitly cloaked in religious language have entirely secular analogues—but that some relationship can at least be claimed is borne out by the express declarations of the perpetrators themselves and by their leaders.[3] By contrast, the sinister fantasies of world domination by "Jewish capitalism" or "Jewish communism" disseminated by the "Protocols of the Elders of Zion" or *Der Stürmer* did not find even remote echoes in the official or unofficial language of Jewish religious leaders. And even when the noose began to tighten around the neck of European Jewry in the 1930s, it is startling how few acts of violence were provoked among the persecuted. There were no shattered office buildings, no bombs in cafes and train stations, no buses blown to pieces on busy streets, no crowds nervously eyeing anyone with a backpack or an ominously thick coat.

Jews in the sixteenth century routinely called upon God to avenge their injuries at the hands of the *goyim*. Then, as now, the Passover Haggadah incorporated the bitter verses of Psalm 79:

> Pour out Your wrath upon the nations which do not know You,
> And upon the kingdoms which do not call upon Your name.
> For they have devoured Jacob
> And laid waste his habitation.

But the vengeance for which they prayed was the Almighty's. Whatever they felt in their hearts, the inhabitants of the ghetto did not publicly declare their own murderous designs upon Christianity, and they did not in fact pose a threat to the dominant culture. As for Tudor London, there were no Jews, at least none who acknowledged themselves as such, the entire population having been expelled in 1290. Fear of the Jews—alarm that they might be meeting in their synagogues to hatch vicious plots against the innocent—was entirely phantasmatic, as it was, for that matter, in nineteenth-century Russia or twentieth-century Berlin.

Of course, medieval and Renaissance Europeans heard horrible stories about the Jews, and the fact that we now know those stories to have been untrue is obviously irrelevant to their contemporary impact. Marlowe's homicidal Jew of Malta gleefully recalls poisoning wells, among other lurid crimes, and in the course of the play, with the help of his homicidal Muslim sidekick Ithamore, he not only murders all of the inhabitants of a nunnery, including his own daughter, but betrays his entire city to the enemy Turks. And Chaucer's prioress was not alone in rehearsing the myth that Jews routinely murdered Christian children. The myth, often linked to the notion that the victims' blood was used to make Passover matzoh, had sufficient credibility to lead repeatedly to the trial and execution of Jews accused of ritual murder. As late as 1913 the charge was brought against Mendel Beilis in Kiev; Beilis was acquitted, but only when the jury split by a vote of six to six.

One can find the blood libel, the charge that Jews practiced ritual murder in order to consume the blood of their victims, circulating in all its old malevolence on the Internet: a glance at a startlingly anti-Semitic website devoted to Simon of Trent will suffice to convince one of that.[4] Apart from the Web, where it is possible to find *anything*, the old charge against the Jews still surfaces regularly and with more or less official sanction only in the Muslim world. Not many years ago, the government-controlled Saudi daily *Al-Riyadh* published a column declaring that "the Jews' spilling human blood to prepare pastry for their holidays is a well-established fact." For Purim, the author, who is affiliated with a respectable Saudi university, informed readers, the victim must be a mature adolescent who is either a Christian or a Muslim; for Passover, children under ten must be used.[5]

In the late sixteenth century it would certainly have been possible for Shakespeare to exploit such lurid stories—after all, he had already tried a human pastry in *Titus Andronicus*—but he chose not to do so. Shylock is a threat to the Christian community of Venice, but the threat has nothing to do with ritual murder. It has rather to do with the nature of his hatred of the dominant culture, his gnawing feeling of injury, and his consequent plotting of revenge. Given Shakespeare's lack of interest in the ancient anti-Jewish libels—there is no mention of poisoned wells, let alone the making of matzoh with Christian blood—he could have depicted Shylock's seething hatred as entirely his own, a pathology akin to that of Aaron the Moor, or the hunchback Richard, or honest Iago. None of these villains represents an entire group; each is driven by something peculiar to himself. To be sure, the criminal drive always exists in some relation to its possessor's whole life, a life that invariably includes group identifications. But the hatred that impels these characters is what pulls each of them out of the larger sociological category and makes them distinctive.

Shakespeare was fascinated by such radical individuation-through-loathing and generally found it sufficient to motivate the action of a play. Aaron is not a murderer, unredeemed and unredeemable, because he is black; indeed, the only lovable quality in him is his defense of his baby—"Sweet blowze, you are a beauteous blossom, sure" (4.2.72)—against the racist slurs of the nurse. Richard at one moment attributes his criminal pathology to his crooked spine, but we are not meant to conclude that all hunchbacks are murderers. And the audience does not have to suspect all ensigns of harboring implacable malice just because Iago does.

"You shall mark," Iago witheringly observes,

> Many a duteous and knee-crooking knave
> That, doting on his own obsequious bondage,
> Wears out his time much like his master's ass
> For naught but provender, and when he's old, cashiered.
> (*Othello* 1.1.44–48)

Such is the caste to which Iago officially belongs, but he will not accept the designation. His hatred is precisely what enables him to escape from it and to mark out what he calls his "peculiar end":

> Heaven is my judge, not I for love and duty,
> But seeming so for my peculiar end.
> For when my outward action doth demonstrate
> The native act and figure of my heart
> In compliment extern, 'tis not long after
> But I will wear my heart upon my sleeve
> For daws to peck at. I am not what I am. (1.1.59–65)

"I am not what I am" is Iago's radical declaration of independence from any group to which his birth and career may have assigned him.

Shylock's villainy is similarly his own, but it is also deeply, essentially implicated in his Jewishness, a Jewishness that serves as a collective principle of negation. Take away Iago's rage at being passed over for promotion and you would still have Iago; take away Richard's deformity, important though it is, and you would still have the twisted mind of the evil duke of Gloucester. Both would, we can be certain, find other grounds, if the need arose, on which to base their murderous designs. After all, Iago is not appeased when he gets his coveted promotion, any more than Richard stops contriving murder when he discovers that he can, after all, seduce a woman. But take away Shylock's Jewishness, and he shrivels into nothingness. That shriveling away is indeed what happens at the end of the fourth act of *The Merchant of Venice*.

There is one group identity in Shakespeare that comes close to Jewishness in its power to motivate resentment and villainy. Edmund's actions in *King Lear* are directly related to the sufferings of an entire class of people—illegitimate children:

> Wherefore should I
> Stand in the plague of custom, and permit
> The curiosity of nations to deprive me,
> For that I am some twelve or fourteen moonshines
> Lag of a brother? Why bastard? wherefore base?
> When my dimensions are as well compact,
> My mind as generous and my shape as true,
> As honest madam's issue? Why brand they us
> With base? with baseness? bastardy? base, base?
> Who, in the lusty stealth of nature, take
> More composition and fierce quality
> Than doth, within a dull, stale, tired bed,
> Go to creating a whole tribe of fops,
> Got 'tween asleep and wake? (1.2.2–15)

Edmund's villainy is the consequence of the social branding against which he rails; to this extent he resembles Shylock. But, unlike Shylock, Edmund is determined to escape as fast as he can from the stigmatized group to which his birth has condemned him. His nature does not express his group identification but rebels against it. And though he commits appalling crimes, Edmund is not actually a hater, in the way that Shylock is. He connives against his brother and his father not because he hates either of them—if anything, he holds them in a kind of perversely affectionate contempt—but rather because he refuses to stay in the collective category assigned to him by his fate.

Contrast Shylock's response, when invited to dine with Bassanio and Antonio:

> Yes, to smell pork, to eat of the habitation which your prophet the Nazarite conjured the devil into! I will buy with you, sell with you, talk with you, walk with you, and so following, but I will not eat with you, drink with you, nor pray with you. (1.3.28–32)

Neither the quarto editions nor the folio indicate whether these words are directed aloud to Bassanio or are an aside. They could be played either way, though it would have been dangerous at the time for a Jew to mention Jesus. In any case, they are manifestly the expression not only of Shylock's personal refusal of social, as distinct from economic, interaction with the gentiles—a refusal that he later contradicts, to his great cost—but also of his Jewish identification. Jewish existence in Venice is only in part defined by Christian laws, the laws that historically compelled Jews to live in the ghetto and restricted the scope of their economic activity, forcing them to be moneylenders. It is also defined by the internal codes of the Jewish community, codes that Shakespeare understands to focus on dietary laws and on prayer. Observing kashrut, Shylock's words make clear, means that Jews must separate themselves from the ordinary fellowship of the gentiles. The words capture something else, something I vividly recall from my own religiously observant parents: a disgust at the very thought of eating pork. I doubt that my parents knew that Jesus had conjured devils into the Gadarene swine, but they felt intensely that the animal was unclean, and they shared the sense that even the smell was vaguely tainted.

Shylock's disgust is not, then, like Edmund's "Why brand they us," a protest against his condition: it *is* his condition, his fundamental identity. He does not want out; he wants to remain in this identity. He is aware of the Christian life around him. He knows that the gentiles eat pork, that they like "the vile squealing of the wry-necked fife," that they amuse themselves by assuming "varnished faces," that is, masks (2.5.29, 32). He is not ignorant of their pleasures; he simply does not want any part of them. He has even read the gentiles' Scriptures, or perhaps has heard them in the sermons that Jews were on occasion forced to attend. Hence his remark about the Nazarite's conjuring or, a moment later, when he glimpses Antonio, his allusion to the publican from chapter 18 of Luke's gospel:

> How like a fawning publican he looks.
> I hate him for he is a Christian;
> But more, for that in low simplicity
> He lends out money gratis, and brings down
> The rate of usance here with us in Venice.
> If I can catch him once upon the hip
> I will feed fat the ancient grudge I bear him.
> He hates our sacred nation, and he rails,
> Even there where merchants most do congregate,
> On me, my bargains, and my well-won thrift—
> Which he calls interest. Cursèd be my tribe
> If I forgive him. (1.3.36–47)

Shylock's hatred of Antonio has an economic motivation—"He lends out money gratis"—but even this determination to protect a personal interest ("me, my bargains, and my well-won thrift") is directly linked to Shylock's fundamental sense of an absolute difference between Christians and "our sacred nation," "my tribe."

"I hate him for he is a Christian." It is as simple or as complicated as that. These are not words spoken to anyone but himself: "Shylock, do you hear?" says Bassanio, noticing that the moneylender is lost in his own thoughts. Those thoughts center on Christian-hating. Of course, Shylock immediately adds an economic motive that he says is even more important, but the economic motive is hardly separable from the collective hatred. After all, Antonio's interest-free loans are a direct assault upon the Jews: "He lends out money gratis, and brings down / The rate of usance here with *us* in Venice." When Iago starts adding to the reasons he hates Othello, the accumulation of motives, each pulling in a different direction, begins to mystify the deep source of his grudge. In *The Merchant of Venice* the motives reinforce each other, and all lead back to Jewish hatred of Christians, "the ancient grudge" that Shylock says he bears.

The grudge is personal—it has a history of direct and extremely ugly encounters:

> You call me misbeliever, cut-throat, dog,
> And spit upon my Jewish gaberdine,
> And all for use of that which is mine own.
> Well then, it now appears you need my help.
> Go to, then. You come to me, and you say
> 'Shylock, we would have moneys'—you say so,
> You, that did void your rheum upon my beard,
> And foot me as you spurn a stranger cur
> Over your threshold. (1.3.107–15)

But this is not a story of personal antipathy alone. The grudge is "ancient" not merely because Antonio has for years spat upon and cursed Shylock; it extends back much further than that, through the long, painful centuries of Jewish-Christian relations. For the Jews those relations have led to the ghetto and an economic life restricted to moneylending and the gabardine with the yellow badge. For the Christians they have led to the behavior that Antonio, ordinarily generous, loving, and somewhat depressive by nature, manifests toward the despised enemy, as if he felt compelled to act out a collective loathing. Shylock's response to this outrageous treatment is, by his own account, also a manifestation of collective behavior:

> Still have I borne it with a patient shrug,
> For suff'rance is the badge of all our tribe. (1.3.105–6)

Shylock, though, stands out from that tribe. He does not bear everything with a patient shrug; he secretly plots revenge, and he does so on his own initiative.[6] That is, he contrives what he calls the "merry bond" with Antonio out of his own head and not in a conspiracy with his fellow Jews (1.3.169). But unlike Richard, Iago, or Edmund, Shylock is not isolated: Shakespeare goes out of his way to identify him with the larger Jewish community within which he lives. The play, which depicts him as a rich man, could easily have shown him acting entirely on his own: the gold and jewels and ducats that his daughter Jessica steals from him, when she runs away with Lorenzo, provide ample evidence of the great wealth he has stored up in his house. Yet in his transaction with Antonio, Shylock immediately involves another Jew. "I am debating of my present store," he says, when he is approached for the loan,

> And by the near guess of my memory
> I cannot instantly raise up the gross
> Of full three thousand ducats. What of that?
> Tubal, a wealthy Hebrew of my tribe,
> Will furnish me. (1.3.48–53)

Why does Shakespeare add this plot wrinkle? It would make sense if Shylock then used Tubal's involvement as an excuse to increase the rate of interest he is charging Antonio, but no such strategy is revealed. Instead Shylock declares that he is offering his Christian tormentor an interest-free loan. "I would be friends with you, and have your love," he tells Antonio,

> Forget the shames that you have stained me with,
> Supply your present wants, and take no doit
> Of usance for my moneys. (1.3.133–36)

All he asks as security for this exceptionally kind offer is a zany pledge whose significance is its complete worthlessness:

> let the forfeit
> Be nominated for an equal pound
> Of your fair flesh to be cut off and taken
> In what part of your body pleaseth me. (1.3.144–47)

What is the point then of bringing in Tubal? The point is that in some sense the loan comes from the tribe as a whole; it is Jewish money. Hence Tubal's later role in the search for Shylock's daughter. ("Here comes another of the tribe," remarks Solanio, when he catches sight of Tubal coming to report to Shylock on the progress of that search [3.1.65].) The elopement is not Shylock's concern alone; it is a tribal concern. And hence too, when the enraged Shylock sees his chance to destroy Antonio, the brief, sinister glimpse out beyond the two Jews to the larger community:

> Go, Tubal, fee me an officer. Bespeak him a fortnight before. I will have the heart of him if he forfeit, for were he out of Venice I can make what merchandise I will. Go, Tubal, and meet me at our synagogue. Go, good Tubal; at our synagogue, Tubal. (3.1.104–8)

"*I* can make what merchandise *I* will"—Shylock is speaking for himself here, not for his fellow Jews. The play has just made clear the reason for this apparent isolation: it is not that Shylock has separated himself from his community but rather that he has

THE LIMITS OF HATRED :: 65

never until this moment fully acknowledged, in his own person, his identification with it. "The curse never fell upon our nation till now," he tells Tubal, and then corrects himself: "I never felt it till now" (3.1.72–73). The long history of Jewish suffering and loss becomes his personal history:

> Why thou, loss upon loss: the thief gone with so much, and so much to find the thief, and no satisfaction, no revenge, nor no ill luck stirring but what lights o' my shoulders, no sighs but o' my breathing, no tears but o' my shedding. (3.1.78–81)

This is narcissistic and self-pitying, but it is not an attempt to pull away from being Jewish. It is rather an attempt to make himself the complete, the quintessential Jew. We are in effect watching the fashioning of full ethnic or religious identification, as if Shylock, by virtue of his prosperity and his entrepreneurial energy, had until now held himself aloof from the communal account of what it meant to be Jewish.

Shylock had already, a few moments earlier, assumed precisely this collective identity in his bitter exchange with Solanio and Salerio. The exchange takes the form of a litany of mocking questions put to Shylock by the two Christians:

> How now, Shylock, what news among the merchants?

> Out upon it, old carrion, rebels it at these years?

> But tell us, do you hear whether Antonio have had any loss at sea or no?

> Why, I am sure if he forfeit thou wilt not take his flesh. What's that good for? (3.1.19–20, 31, 35–36, 43–44)

Increasingly exasperated by the mockery, Shylock responds with a question of his own, to which he himself provides the answer:

He hath disgraced me, and hindered me half a million; laughed
at my losses, mocked at my gains, scorned my nation, thwarted
my bargains, cooled my friends, heated mine enemies, and what's
his reason?—I am a Jew. (3.1.46–49)

"I am a Jew"—these four simple words are at once Antonio's "reason," the explanation for his behavior toward Shylock, and Shylock's affirmation of his own identity.[7] And it is out of this basic,
apparently irreducible affirmation that Shylock spins out the famous questions that follow:

Hath not a Jew eyes? Hath not a Jew hands, organs, dimensions,
senses, affections, passions; fed with the same food, hurt with
the same weapons, subject to the same diseases, healed by the
same means, warmed and cooled by the same winter and summer
as a Christian is? If you prick us do we not bleed? If you tickle
us do we not laugh? If you poison us do we not die? And if you
wrong us shall we not revenge? (3.1.49–56)

To insist that Jews are human only makes sense in the context of
suspicion that they might *not* be, that they might be something
else. What it is that they might be instead is disclosed immediately after, in words that indicate that Salerio and Solanio have
not after all been persuaded by Shylock's catechism:

Here comes another of the tribe. A third cannot be matched unless the devil himself turn Jew. (3.1.65–66)

The devil is the great Enemy whom the Jews incarnate and whom
the good Antonio is obliged as a Christian to hate with all his
heart and soul.

Shylock's words are a declaration of his identity—"I am a
Jew"—and at the same time an attempt to refuse this phantas-
magorical equation of his identity with the metaphysical enemy
that late-medieval Christianity perceived in Jews and Jewish-

ness.[8] Hence his peculiar, passionate emphasis on shared bodily being: eyes, hands, bleeding, laughing, and so forth. The insistence on the common humanity that links Jews and gentiles leads Shylock to forget crucial marks of difference—circumcision, of course, along with one of the key distinctions on which he himself had earlier insisted: we are "fed with the same food," he now says. The idea here is not fellowship, of course; it is enmity, as he freely concedes, but it is political enmity, not the dream of absolute, indelible, ineradicable otherness.

And yet it is precisely that dream that Shylock acts out in the courtroom. Implacable, unappeasable, vicious, he sharpens the knife he intends to use to cut out a pound of Antonio's flesh, for "by our holy Sabbath," he declares, "have I sworn /To have the due and forfeit of my bond" (4.1.35–36). Antonio underscores what this oath discloses: the specifically Jewish character of Shylock's determination. "You may as well do anything most hard," the victim bound for slaughter declares,

> As seek to soften that—than which what's harder?—
> His Jewish heart. (4.1.77–79)

The intemperate Graziano is "too wild, too rude and bold of voice" (2.2.162), as his friend Bassanio puts it, to be taken fully seriously, but he is not alone in questioning whether Shylock— "wolvish, bloody, starved, and ravenous" (4.1.137)—is fully human. Entirely untouched by what the duke calls "human gentleness and love" (4.1.24), Shylock seems to embody the limitless, unreasonable, inexplicable hatred that for Christians marked the essential affiliation of the Jews with the father of all evil.

But in fact the long courtroom scene in *The Merchant of Venice* does not end with the revelation that Shylock is the offspring of Satan. It ends rather with the startling disclosure that Shylock's hatred has its limits. To be sure, he does not succumb to Portia's eloquent plea for mercy. "My deeds upon my head!" he insists, but then he adds, "I crave the law" (4.1.201). This craving for the law, here the desire to take Antonio's life in a civil suit, marks the boundary beyond which Shylock dares not go. He has the opportunity to act—a sharp knife in his hand, the naked breast of his loathed enemy exposed and vulnerable, the chance to strike. He is waiting, to be sure, for the judge's express permission, a permission he expects will be granted momentarily, so it does not make sense to strike prematurely. But when Portia discloses the legal wrinkle in the contract—"This bond doth give thee here no jot of blood. / The words expressly are 'a pound of flesh'" (4.1.301–2)—Shylock could still act. Portia makes this option clear in spelling out the consequences:

> Therefore prepare thee to cut off the flesh.
> Shed thou no blood, nor cut thou less nor more
> But just a pound of flesh. If thou tak'st more
> Or less than a just pound, be it but so much
> As makes it light or heavy in the substance
> Or the division of the twentieth part
> Of one poor scruple—nay, if the scale do turn
> But in the estimation of a hair,
> Thou diest, and all thy goods are confiscate. (4.1.319–27)

The confiscation of his goods is beside the point; Shylock's daughter Jessica has already stolen what she could find in his house and run off with a Christian. It is simply his own life that he will have to sacrifice to take his revenge upon Antonio.

"Hates any man the thing he would not kill?" (4.1.66), Shylock had asked.[9] Portia now has devised a test to see how much Shylock hates Antonio, and the answer is not enough. Not enough to plunge the knife into his enemy's heart, which he can do at this very moment, in the sight of all those who have mocked and despised him, provided he is willing to die for it. Faced with the demand of such absolute, suicidal hatred, Shylock flinches: "Give me my principal, and let me go" (4.1.331).

Instead of pursuing hatred to its ultimate end—the longed-for annihilation of his enemy at the simple cost of self-slaughter—the Jew makes a different choice: he opts for his money ("Give me my principal") and his life ("let me go"). At first he asks for what only a few moments earlier Bassanio has offered to pay: "Yea, twice the sum. If that will not suffice / I will be bound to pay it ten times o'er" (4.1.205–6). But when this extravagant interest is now refused, he asks only for the sum he has originally advanced—"barely my principal" (4.1.337)—and in doing so he makes clear that he is attempting to secure the means for his survival: "you take my life / When you do take the means whereby I live" (4.1.371–72).

At the decisive moment of his life, the Christian Antonio, prepared for martyrdom, had asked that all attempts at further negotiation with Shylock be dropped—"I do beseech you, / Make no more offers" (4.1.79–80)—and had expressed his complete willingness to die:

> I am a tainted wether of the flock,
> Meetest for death. The weakest kind of fruit
> Drops earliest to the ground; and so let me. (4.1.113–15).

At his comparably decisive moment, the Jew Shylock seems by constrast to hear the words of Deuteronomy: "Therefore choose life" (30:19). But it is not so simple, as Portia quickly reveals.

Shylock wanted to stay within the embrace of the law, and the embrace now closes in upon him. Since the Jew has in effect sought to take the life of a Venetian citizen, the case has shifted from a civil to a criminal matter and the plaintiff has become the defendant. Antonio sets the terms of the settlement that enables Shylock to escape execution: the immediate loss of half his goods, his entire estate to go to his daughter and her husband, and his conversion to Christianity, that is, the loss of difference. And with this loss of difference, the Jew simply disappears. The play still has an entire act before it reaches its end. All that is left is comedy, tinged with melancholy to be sure, but nonetheless comedy.

Shylock's conversion and disappearance, which redeems a play that had veered perilously close to tragedy, marks the point at which the specific, bounded cultural mobility with which I began this essay breaks down. That mobility depended, I have suggested, not on a pure, abstract logic of substitution but on the special link between Christianity's two apocalyptic and hence radically unassimilable enemies, Judaism and Islam. Shakespeare's aesthetic solution lies in an assimilation to which the enemy finally consents because the alternative is to lose his life and his livelihood. Faced with the prospect of such a loss, Shylock reaches the limits of his hatred.

Some years after Shakespeare wrote *The Merchant of Venice* he returned to the subject of hatred and tried to imagine what it would be like if the hater did not accept any limits, if he were willing to go as far as he had to go to destroy his enemy. The play once again deals with outsiders and insiders, but now the great hater is one of the insiders.[10] Iago is not interested in justice; he does not crave the law. He desires only Othello's utter ruin, and he will stop at nothing to bring it about. It does not matter that he is dependent on Othello, first as ensign and then as lieutenant, the position he coveted; it does not matter that his wife Emilia is the lady maid of Othello's wife Desdemona. One of the ironies of Iago's celebrated advice, "Put money in thy purse" (first at 1.3.333), is that he himself is entirely uninterested in his own well-being. Hatred as intense and single-minded as his is finally indifferent to his very survival.

Near the play's end, when Othello finally understands what he has been gulled into doing, he stares at Iago in astonishment: "I look down towards his feet," he says, expecting to see the cloven hooves that would confirm the demonic origins of such evil. But the magical clarity that revelation would bring is not forthcom-

ing: "I look down towards his feet, but that's a fable" (5.2.292).
What Othello sees instead is the body of a man. "Will you, I pray,
demand that demi-devil," he asks, holding onto a shred of the fable, "Why he hath thus ensnared my soul and body?" (5.2.307–8).
To a comparable question in *The Merchant of Venice* Shylock replies that he can give no reason other than "a lodged hate and a
certain loathing" (4.1.59) that he bears Antonio. In *Othello* Iago
refuses even the minimal satisfaction that such a stripped-down
declaration of motive could provide:

> Demand me nothing. What you know, you know.
> From this time forth I never will speak word. (5.2.309–10)

There is no comic potential on the other side of this moment, no
escape to the moonlit garden in the country house. In the face
of a limitless, absolute, wordless hatred lodged in an ordinary
human being, the bystanders are reduced to incoherence. One
of them talks about torturing Iago in order to open his lips and
make him speak—but what is the point? The audience has heard
everything Iago has to say and knows that nothing he could reveal under torture will help. It is this knowledge, along with the
knowledge that the demi-devil is altogether human, that gives
weight to the word used at the play's end to describe the spectacle of bodies piled on the bed, a word that for once has its full,
resonant force: tragic.

"Look on the tragic loading of this bed," the Venetian official Lodovico tells Iago, "This is thy work" (5.2.373–74). Part of
the resonance of "tragic" here is its glancing acknowledgment of
the specifically literary quality of what Iago has brought forth,
and hence a covert, painful acknowledgment of the extent of
the playwright's identification with his most terrifying villain.
Shakespeare identified with Shylock as well—a fine recent book
on *The Merchant of Venice* is entitled *Shylock Is Shakespeare* [11]—
but the limits of that identification are clearly marked by the

theatrical life that continues for an entire act on the other side of Shylock's disappearance. On the far side of Iago's disappearance, there is only silence.

Shakespeare's comedy offered the audience a reassuring, if uneasy, fantasy of conversion: Shylock would become one of us, and in doing so he would disappear. But there is no comparable reassurance in Othello: honest Iago's hatred has no limits, and he is already one of us.

In the face of this unbearable fact, Othello, the black outsider who has made himself into the heroic defender of Christian civilization, desperately attempts to secure a crumbling moral world. "I have done the state some service," he declares, "and they know't" (5.2.348). There was a time at which such a declaration might have rung out with a particular ethical force, the force that derives from putting off personal considerations in order to serve a grand collective enterprise.[12] But the storm that scattered the Ottoman fleet has drained away the sense of purpose that gives authority its confident sense of self-justification and importance.

The Venetian officials who speak at the end of *Othello*, Graziano and Lodovico, make all the gestures appropriate to the restoration of public order:

> You must forsake this room and go with us.
> Your power and your command is taken off,
> And Cassio rules in Cyprus. . . .
> . . . You shall close prisoner rest.
> . . . Come, bring away. (5.2.339–46)

But the authority of the Venetian state to judge and punish and redistribute property—the authority that settled affairs in *The Merchant of Venice*—seems at the end of *Othello* to have lost all moral meaning. Does anyone care that Othello's house and wealth, whatever it amounts to, is given at the end to Desdemona's uncle Graziano? And the renewed call for the torture of Iago—"O, enforce it!" (5.2.379)—seems only to reinforce the sense of the state's irrelevance in the face of fathomless hatred.

Graziano and Lodovico take conventional steps to reassure themselves that the situation is now under control. They register the horror of what has happened, but they cannot bear to contemplate it for more than a few moments. They ready themselves to return home, where they will make their report—without actually understanding anything. Confronted by the evidence of incomprehensible, limitless, suicidal malevolence, they do what most of us do in order to get on with our ordinary, genially incoherent lives: they draw the curtain. "The object poisons sight./Let it be hid" (5.2.374–75).

It falls to Othello, always prone to heroic actions, to try on his own to reconstitute shattered ethical authority. For the all-too-human Iago there is no redemption, nor will anything that Othello or anyone else does succeed in bringing Desdemona back to life. But through the fog of his confusion and grief, Othello sees a way both to regain control over what he had called the story of his life and to repair the damage that had been done to the authority of the state he had loyally served. He can do so by personally dragging Iago's actions back into the orbit of the community and its ends. Honest Iago, the perfect insider, had seemed to exemplify that community's values, but he had in fact betrayed them into nihilism: "I am not what I am." Othello's task is to identify and destroy an appropriate enemy, a target that the Venetian Christians had long deemed worthy of hatred.

Othello finds this target in himself. He likens himself first to the "base Judean" who threw away a pearl worth all his tribe,[13] and then, as if this Jewishness were not enough to elicit loathing without limits, he turns to the other great enemy—"a malignant and a turbaned Turk"—and rises to a final, suicidal assault upon them both: "I took by th' throat the circumcisèd dog/And smote him thus" (5.2.356, 362, 364–65).[14]

Shakespeare and the Ethics of Authority

In 1998, a friend of mine, Robert Pinsky, who at the time was serving as poet laureate of the United States, invited me to a poetry evening at the White House, one of a series of black-tie events organized to mark the coming millennium. On this occasion President Clinton gave an introductory speech in which he recalled that his first encounter with poetry came in junior high school when his teacher made him memorize certain passages from *Macbeth*. This was, he remarked wryly, not the most auspicious beginning for a life in politics.

After the speeches, I joined the line waiting to shake the president's hand. When my turn came, a strange impulse came over me. This was a moment when rumors of the Lewinsky affair were circulating but before the whole thing had blown up into the grotesque national circus that it soon became. "Mr. President," I said, sticking out my hand, "Don't you think that *Macbeth* is a great play about an immensely ambitious man who feels compelled to do things that he knows are politically and morally disastrous?" Clinton looked at me for a moment, still holding my hand, and said, "I think *Macbeth* is a great play about someone whose immense ambition has an ethically inadequate object."

I was astonished by the aptness, as well as the quickness, of this comment, so perceptively in touch with Macbeth's anguished brooding about the impulses that are driving him to seize power by murdering Scotland's legitimate ruler:

> I have no spur
> To prick the sides of my intent, but only
> Vaulting ambition which o'erleaps itself
> And falls on th'other. (1.7.25–28)

I left the White House that evening with the thought that Bill Clinton had missed his true vocation, which was, of course, to be an English professor. But the profession he actually chose makes it all the more appropriate to consider whether it is possible in Shakespeare to discover an "ethically adequate object" for human ambition.

Macbeth himself seems tormented by the question. To be sure, his anxiety derives in part from a straightforward prudential concern, a fear that what he metes out will inevitably be meted out to him, measure for measure. But his queasiness has deeper roots in his sense of ethical obligation, in this case the obligation to obey and serve the king his master. His wife, who knows her husband's character all too well, has already cannily anticipated his inner struggle:

> Thou wouldst be great,
> Art not without ambition, but without
> The illness should attend it. (1.5.16–18)

Hence, faced with the perfect opportunity to seize the crown—King Duncan is a guest in his castle—Macbeth holds back. He is, he reflects, Duncan's kinsman and subject, and at this moment he is also the king's host, "Who should against his murderer shut the door, / Not bear the knife myself" (1.7.15–16). Above all, there has been nothing in the king's comportment that would make his murder a remotely justifiable act. (Shakespeare characteristically altered his source, eliding evidence of Duncan's incompetence and thus eliminating a rational basis for his assassination.) On the contrary, Macbeth broods,

> this Duncan
> Hath borne his faculties so meek, hath been
> So clear in his great office, that his virtues
> Will plead like angels, trumpet-tongued against
> The deep damnation of his taking-off. (1.7.16–20)

"Meek" is a strange word to describe a king whom we have just seen conducting a bloody military campaign and ordering the summary execution of his enemy, the thane of Cawdor. But it serves to intensify Macbeth's brooding on the "deep damnation" that will befall Duncan's assassin.

The theological language here must, I think, be understood as an expression of the would-be assassin's inner fears and not as Shakespeare's own affirmation of the sacredness of kingship. From time to time, of course, we hear such affirmations in his work, but they tend to be treated with deft irony:

> There's such divinity doth hedge a king
> That treason can but peep to what it would.

Those stirring words are spoken by the regicide Claudius, successfully pacifying the enraged Laertes (*Hamlet* 4.5.120–21). None of Shakespeare's plays, not even *Macbeth*, unequivocally endorses the view that every act of usurpation is automatically evil, and none condemns as necessarily unethical the use of violence to topple the established order. Unlike the most conservative voices in his time, Shakespeare did not position himself squarely against the bloody unthroning even of anointed monarchs. Violence, as he well understood, was one of the principal mechanisms of regime change.

Richard III, to take an example from early in Shakespeare's career, has royal blood and a better lineal claim to the throne than anyone in the realm. (To be sure, he has seen to that by murdering everyone in his way, but ruthlessness was never strictly incompatible with legitimacy.) He is careful to wrap himself in the mantle of moral authority, appearing before the citizens with prayer book in hand in the company of two "deep divines" (3.7.75), and if this show of piety is hypocritical and the popular acclamation manipulated, Shakespeare's audience easily grasped that such shows were essential elements in the order of things. Some might have still recalled that Queen Elizabeth ostentatiously kissed a bible during her coronation procession. Yet Shakespeare's history play never doubts that it is reasonable, sane, even necessary, to rise up on the side of the usurper. The beleaguered king vigorously exhorts his troops to destroy the invading army, "vagabonds, rascals and runaways" led by a "paltry fellow" (5.6.46, 53). But the paltry fellow succeeds in killing the king.

Yet even if Shakespeare treated the mystical accounts of kingship with relentless irony, he did not endorse any general principle of resistance. Such principles were readily available in a variety of forms: the tyrannicide advocated by George Buchanan; the passive disobedience proposed by Montaigne's friend Etienne de la Boétie; the oligarchical republicanism articulated by Thomas Starkey. "What is more repugnant to nature," Starkey wrote during the reign of Henry VIII, "than a whole nation to be governed by the will of a prince, which ever followeth his frail fantasy and unruled affects?"[1] The only way to secure the well-being, dignity, and liberty of men, he declared, was to hold free elections, the means that had fashioned the greatness of the ancient Roman republic and that accounted in his view for the flourishing success of contemporary Venice.

Shakespeare, deeply invested imaginatively in both Rome and Venice, understood this argument very well, yet he kept a critical, ironic distance from it. There are elections in his work—in *Titus Andronicus*, for example, and in *Coriolanus, Hamlet,* and *Macbeth*—but they are all deeply flawed. It is not that the plays are sentimental about the alternative to elections: they offer many variations on a spectacle epitomized by *Julius Caesar,* sur-

rounded by cynical flatterers, caught up in his own cult of person-
ality, and poised to destroy the tottering liberties of Rome. The
republican conspirators who determine to rid themselves of this
public menace adhere to a moral principle: "I was born free as
Caesar," Cassius tells Brutus; "so were you" (1.2.99). But it is not
clear that they themselves have the will to govern; indeed, Brutus
makes clear in his oration that it was precisely the manifestation
of this will in Caesar that prompted his murder:

> As Caesar loved me, I weep for him. As he was fortunate, I re-
> joice at it. As he was valiant, I honour him. But as he was ambi-
> tious, I slew him. (3.2.23–25)

If the conspirators nonetheless aim to wield power in the newly
restored Roman republic, that aim, as the play shows, is doomed
by their own internecine disagreements, their contempt for the
will of the people, and their fatal errors of judgment. At the close
the triumphant Antony briefly pauses to pay homage to what he
calls Brutus's "general honest thought," that is, his ethical motivation—

> All the conspirators save only he
> Did that they did in envy of great Caesar.
> He only in a general honest thought
> And common good to all made one of them. (5.5.68–71)

Then he and Octavius turn to the serious business of carving up
the Roman state.

Brutus's fate is not his alone: in Shakespeare *no* character with
a clear moral vision has a will to power and, conversely, no character with a strong desire to rule over others has an ethically
adequate object. This is most obviously true of Shakespearean
villains—the megalomaniac Richard III, the bastard Edmund
(along with the ghastly Goneril, Regan, and Cornwall), the
Macbeths, and the like—but it is also true of such characters

as Bolingbroke in the *Henry IV* plays, Cassius in *Julius Caesar,* Fortinbras in *Hamlet,* and Malcolm in *Macbeth.* Even victorious Henry V—Shakespeare's most charismatic hero—does not substantially alter the plays' overarching skepticism about the ethics of wielding authority.

No one is more aware than the reformed wastrel, Henry V, that there is something deeply flawed in his whole possession of power and in the foreign war he has cynically launched on the flimsiest of pretexts. On the eve of the decisive battle of Agincourt, he queasily negotiates a settlement with God—"Not today, O Lord, / O not today, think not upon the fault / My father made in compassing the crown" (4.1.274–76)—and evidently God is at least temporarily won over. But, as the epilogue makes clear, the king's son and successor was soon to lose everything that his father had won. And the irony is that this son, Henry VI, is virtually the only Shakespearean ruler with a high-minded, ethical goal: a deeply religious man, he is passionately committed to bringing peace among his fractious, violent, and blindly ambitious nobles. Unfortunately, this pious king has no skills at governance whatever. The nobles easily destroy him and plunge the realm into a bloody civil war.

Henry V is probably the closest Shakespeare ever came to representing the authority of the ruler as divinely sanctioned. At the end of the play the triumphant Henry proclaims the death penalty for anyone who denies that the victory was God's alone. But the proclamation only underscores what the play repeatedly makes clear: here, as throughout Shakespeare's work, the ethics of authority are deeply compromised.

All of Shakespeare's histories and tragedies end with an affirmation of order restored, and the order is on occasion dressed in moral robes:

> Now civil wounds are stopped; peace lives again.
> That she may long live here, God say 'Amen'.
> (*Richard 3* 5.8.40–41)

I'll make a voyage to the Holy Land
To wash this blood off from my guilty hand.
(*Richard 2* 5.6.49–50)
    this and what needful else
That calls upon us, by the grace of grace
We will perform in measure, time, and place.
(*Macbeth* 5.11.37–39)

But the robes, by design, never quite fit. The state at the close of virtually every one of these plays is what Albany calls a "gored state" (*King Lear* 5.3.319), and the ability to survive the wounds has little or nothing to do with ethical values.

If one seeks genuine skills at governance in Shakespeare, they are most attractively on display in Claudius, the usurper in *Hamlet* who kills his brother, Hamlet's father, to become king:

Thus much the business is: we have here writ
To Norway, uncle of young Fortinbras—
Who, impotent and bed-rid, scarcely hears
Of this his nephew's purpose—to suppress
His further gait herein, in that the levies,
The lists, and full proportions are all made
Out of his subject; and we here dispatch
You, good Cornelius, and you, Valtemand,
For bearers of this greeting to old Norway,
Giving to you no further personal power
To business with the King more than the scope
Of these dilated articles allow.
Farewell, and let your haste commend your duty. (1.2.27–39)

Shakespeare risked this uncharacteristically dull speech in order to convey the voice of authority: businesslike, confident, decisive, careful, and politically astute. And it is, of course, the voice of a murderer, the festering source of all that is rotten in the state of Denmark.

It is those who attempt to pull back from power who fascinated Shakespeare at least as much as those who strive to exercise it: the spoiled dreamer, Richard II, who seems to embrace his fall from the throne; the love-crazed Antony, who prefers embracing Cleopatra to ruling the world; Coriolanus, who cannot abide the ordinary rituals of political life; and old Lear, who hopes

> To shake all cares and business from our age,
> Conferring them on younger strengths, while we
> Unburthened crawl toward death. (1.1.37–39)

What all of these very different characters have in common—and we could add Duke Vincentio in *Measure for Measure* and Prospero in *The Tempest*—is the desire to escape from the burdens of governance. In each case, the desire leads to disaster.

For if Shakespeare was drawn to those who want to walk away from positions of authority, he was at the same time convinced that this attempt is doomed. Power exists to be exercised in the world. It will not go away if you close your eyes and dream of escaping into your study or your lover's arms or your daughter's house. It will simply be seized by someone else, probably someone more coldly efficient than you and still further from an ethically adequate object: Bolingbroke, Octavius Caesar, Edmund, Angelo, Prospero's usurping brother Antonio.

"Rapt in secret studies" (*Tempest* 1.2.77), Prospero loses his dukedom, but even in exile he does not escape the authority to which he was culpably indifferent. Instead he finds himself, together with his daughter, on an island that serves as a kind of laboratory for testing the ethics of authority. Prospero possesses many of the princely virtues that the Renaissance prized, but the results of the experiment are at best deeply ambiguous: one of the island's native inhabitants is liberated only to be forced into compulsory servitude; the other is educated only to be enslaved.

Prospero does seem to make one crucial ethical breakthrough: though his hated brother and his other enemies come to be under his absolute control, he chooses not to exact vengeance upon them. But this choice is made at the urging of the spirit Ariel, who declares what he would do "were I human" (5.1.20). Perhaps the more striking ethical choice that Prospero makes—and on his own, without Ariel's urging—is to give up his magical powers (the romance equivalent of martial law), take back the dukedom he had lost twelve years earlier, and return to the city from which he had been exiled. By doing so he deliberately plunges back into the contingency, risk, and moral uncertainty that he had temporarily escaped. And, tellingly, he leaves Ariel behind.

The conclusion toward which these stories tend is not the cynical abandonment of all hope for decency in public life, but rather a deep skepticism about any attempt to formulate and obey an abstract moral law, independent of actual social, political, and psychological circumstances. This skepticism set Shakespeare at odds with the dominant currents of ethical reflection in his period. It is not that he set out, like Marlowe, to swim against these currents or to stage violent protests against them; he seems simply to have found them incompatible with his art.

Renaissance moral thought, like the Christian theology on which it drew, was deeply influenced by what the philosopher Bernard Williams calls the "ethicized psychology" invented by Plato. The idea, against which Williams's powerful book *Shame and Necessity* struggles, is that "the functions of the mind, above all with regard to action, are defined in terms of categories that get their significance from ethics." Thus psychic conflict, especially that between reason and desire, is mistakenly understood as inevitably an ethical conflict. In this influential but misguided tradition, "reason operates as a distinctive part of the soul," Williams observes, "only to the extent that it controls, dominates, or rises above the desires."[2]

There is a glimpse of this ethicized psychology in *The Tempest,* precisely in Prospero's response to the spirit Ariel's moral advice. "Though with their high wrongs I am struck to th' quick," Prospero says of his enemies,

PLATE 1. Leonardo da Vinci, *Lady with an Ermine* (1485–90). Czartoryski Museum, Cracow. Photo: Nimatallah/Art Resource, NY.

PLATE 2. (Attributed to) Nicholas Hilliard, "Phoenix Portrait" of Elizabeth I (ca. 1575). Photo © National Portrait Gallery, London.

PLATE 3. Master of the Magdalen Legend, *The Five Wounds of Christ* (ca. 1523).

PLATE 4. Hieronymus Bosch, *Christ Mocked* (ca. 1490–1500). Photo ©
National Gallery, London/Art Resource, NY.

Yet with my nobler reason 'gainst my fury
Do I take part. (5.1.25–27)

But the play as a whole—and the great body of work of which it is
a part—resists the idea of a moralized basic structure of the mind
and, with it, the search for an intrinsically just conception of responsibility. Prospero's character is too complex, his relations
with Ariel, Caliban, and the others too fraught, to be mapped
comfortably onto a stable distinction between moral and non-
moral motivations.

If Shakespeare evidently found this distinction untenable, his
problem with it lay in what Williams identifies as its underlying
basis: "a distinctive and false picture of the moral life, according
to which the truly moral self is characterless."[3] For Shakespeare
there was no such thing as a characterless self. His doubts were
rooted in his practice; that is, they were inseparable from his
power as a playwright. A conception of the moral self as characterless was not for Shakespeare a philosophical blunder so much
as an undoing or denial of his life's work.

Shakespeare's characters have a rich and compelling moral
life, but that moral life is not autonomous. In each case it is inti-
mately bound up with the particular and distinct community in
which the character participates. In *Julius Caesar* Brutus thinks
that he is acting on ethical principles, uncompromised by peer
pressure, but the audience knows otherwise. "Well, Brutus, thou
art noble," remarks Cassius to himself:

yet I see
Thy honourable mettle may be wrought
From that it is disposed. (1.2.302–4)

It is Brutus's failure to understand the extent to which he is
"wrought"—his refusal to register the social influences upon him
and his fantasy of absolute ethical autonomy—that dooms him.

It would be possible, I believe, to argue that Shakespeare's tragic vision was the consequence of the political defects of his age. The absence of any conception of democratic institutions and the rule of a hereditary monarch with absolutist pretensions left little or no room to formulate an ethical object for secular ambition. Yet Shakespeare's own skepticism seemed to extend to the popular voice, so ironically treated in *Julius Caesar* and *Coriolanus.* That is, when he tried to imagine electioneering, voting, and representation, he conjured up situations in which people, manipulated by wealthy and fathomlessly cynical politicians, were repeatedly induced to act against their own interests.

Rule in Shakespeare is the fate of those who have been born to it. It is the fate as well of those who have been driven to exercise it out of desperation, forced, like Richmond in *Richard III,* Edgar in *Lear,* or Malcolm in *Macbeth,* to confront an evil so appalling that they have no choice but to act. A relatively small number of other characters, generally born in the proximity of power but not its direct heirs, actively seek to seize the reins of government, and a few of these are ruthless or lucky enough to be successful, but Shakespeare inevitably depicts them as eventually broken by the burden they have shouldered. Perhaps this was for him a peculiar form of consolation or hope.

Governance, as Shakespeare imagines it, is an immense weight, whose great emblem is the insomnia that afflicts the competent, tough-minded usurper Bolingbroke after he has become Henry IV. There are books now that profess to derive principles of governance from Shakespeare's works, but sleeplessness — tormenting, constant sleeplessness — is one of the only principles that he consistently depicts.

There is one other key principle, which will take us back to Bill Clinton's remark about Macbeth. Macbeth dreams of killing his guest, King Duncan, and seizing power. He wants the assassination to be swift, decisive, once-for-all: mission accomplished. "If it were *done* when 'tis done," he puts it, "then 'twere well / It were done quickly" (1.7.1–2; emphasis added). The lure is strong

enough, he says, to make him ignore the threat of divine judgment in the afterlife, but still for a fateful moment he holds back:

> We still have judgement here, that we but teach
> Bloody instructions which, being taught, return
> To plague th' inventor. (1.7.8–10)

This is, I think, Shakespeare's central perception of governance,
and it stands in the place of any more high-minded ethical object.
The actions of those in power have consequences, long-term, inescapable, and impossible to control. "We still have judgement
here." It is not in some imagined other world that your actions
will be judged; it is here and now. Judgment in effect means pun-
ishment: whatever violent or dishonest things you do will serve
as a lesson for others, who will revisit them on you. Shakespeare
did not think that one's good actions are necessarily or even usually rewarded, but he seems to have been convinced that one's
wicked actions inevitably return, with interest.

Even in a play haunted, as *Macbeth* is, by witches and the ghost
of a murdered man, this causal order does not imply supernatural
necessity. There is no position outside the world or outside history from which Shakespeare's characters can authenticate their
actions or secure an abstract, ethically adequate object for their
ambitions. Even the survival of the state does not constitute such
an object. One final, startling example will serve to make the
point. In the wake of Lear's abdication, the Duke of Cornwall
is the legitimate, formally sanctioned ruler of half the kingdom,
and yet the play stages and clearly justifies his assassination. The
attack comes suddenly and without warning as he is going about
the business of statecraft: specifically, he is attempting to extract
from the Earl of Gloucester, by any means necessary, information vital to national security, information about a French army
set upon invasion of the realm.

The audience has already learned what Cornwall does not yet

fully know: that the invasion is well under way. A few scenes earlier, the banished Earl of Kent, in disguise, has taken a gentleman into his confidence. "From France," he whispers,

> there comes a power
> Into this scattered kingdom, who already,
> Wise in our negligence, have secret feet
> In some of our best ports, and are at point
> To show their open banner.
> (*History of King Lear*, scene 8, 21–25)[4]

In league with this power, Kent gives the gentleman a token and instructs him to make haste to Dover where he will report to "Some that will thank you" (*History of King Lear*, scene 8, 28).

Kent is not the only high-level collaborator with the invading army. The Earl of Gloucester too has received word. He tells his son Edmund that "there's part of a power already footed" (3.3.11) and that he intends to help them topple Cornwall's regime. Edmund, however, has his own plans. He gives Cornwall documentary proof of his father's treasonous conspiracy: "This is the letter he spoke of, which approves him an intelligent party to the advantages of France" (3.5.8–9). Edmund is a swine, of course, but the letter is authentic.

When they receive this news, Cornwall and his wife Regan are guests in Gloucester's house. Ordinarily their behavior would be strictly bound by this circumstance, but the state of emergency suspends all customary relations and sets the stage for moral and ethical transgression. Cornwall needs to know, and quickly, whatever Gloucester knows about the foreign invasion and why he has sent the old, mad king to Dover. "Go seek the traitor Gloucester," Cornwall orders his servants. "Pinion him like a thief, bring him before us" (3.7.22–23). Gloucester is duly apprehended and bound to a chair. There follows a tense scene of interrogation, chilling in its realistic representation of bluffing, evasiveness, and desperate urgency:

CORNWALL Come, sir, what letters had you late from France?

REGAN Be simple answered, for we know the truth.

CORNWALL And what confederacy have you with the traitors
    Late footed in the kingdom?

REGAN To whose hands have you sent the lunatic king? Speak.

GLOUCESTER I have a letter guessingly set down,
    Which came from one that's of a neutral heart,
    And not from one opposed.

CORNWALL   Cunning.

REGAN   And false.

CORNWALL Where hast thou sent the king?

GLOUCESTER To Dover.

REGAN Wherefore to Dover? Wast thou not charged at peril—

CORNWALL Wherefore to Dover? —Let him first answer that.

GLOUCESTER I am tied to the stake, and I must stand the course.

REGAN Wherefore to Dover? (*King Lear* 3.7.42–56)

This brilliantly written exchange is almost always left out of critical accounts of this scene because of what immediately follows:
the horrendous blinding of Gloucester by the fiendlike inter-
rogators.

   Shakespeare's audience was far less squeamish about the torture of traitors than we are—or than we Americans were until
recently. The use, for the purposes of extracting information
to protect the state, of the "manacles" (that is, the strappado),
the rack, the thumbscrew, and the horrible device known as the
Scavenger's Daughter was a matter of public knowledge and
general acceptance. The common law of England forbade it, but
both Queen Elizabeth and King James claimed royal prerogative
in ordering its use, upon warrant from the Privy Council.[5] The
victims for the most part were Catholics: Jesuits, stubborn re-
cusants, and conspirators. The 1597 warrant for the Jesuit priest
John Gerard explains that the prisoner "very lately did receive a
packet of letters out of the Low Countries which are supposed
to come out of Spain." The examiners in the Tower are therefore

authorized to interrogate him, "wherein if you shall find him obstinate, undutiful, or unwilling to declare and reveal the truth as he ought to do by his duty and allegiance, you shall by virtue hereof cause him to be put to the manacles and such other torture as is used in that place, that he may be forced to utter directly and truly his uttermost knowledge in all these things that may any way concern her Majesty and the State and are meet to be known."[6] The spectators of *King Lear* would have had no occasion to see such a warrant for themselves, but they had recently had a full lesson in how far the government would go, in the hideous, well-publicized treatment of the Gunpowder conspirator, Guy Fawkes. No one ventured to protest out loud.

In 1610 a company of traveling players in the north of England included *King Lear* among the plays, for the most part exercises in piety, that they performed at the manor house of a Catholic couple, Sir John and Lady Julyan Yorke. Both the playing company and its hosts were denounced for recusancy to the Star Chamber. Someone then, during Shakespeare's lifetime, clearly believed that *King Lear,* though set in pre-Christian Britain, was somehow sympathetic to the plight of persecuted Catholics. The link is not immediately apparent to modern readers, but in the scene of Gloucester's blinding we may most clearly sense it. For in *King Lear* Shakespeare contrived to represent the practice of torture in such a way as to make it utterly recognizable—the urgent questioning of someone who has been caught conniving with a foreign power to topple the established regime—and utterly unacceptable.

He did so by collapsing the hygienic distance that separated the monarch and the privy councilors, cloaked in the mantle of moral authority, from the vicious underlings who carried out their orders. Torture in *King Lear* is conducted directly by the rulers, Cornwall and Regan, who are depicted as reptilian monsters. Moreover, Shakespeare subtly uncoupled the infliction of torture from the search for information and hence undermined any simple instrumental rationale. Before Cornwall even gets his hands on the high-born traitor, he declares his intention to injure him, quite apart from the outcome of the process of interrogation:

> Though well we may not pass upon his life
> Without the form of justice, yet our power
> Shall do a courtesy to our wrath, which men
> May blame, but not control. (3.7.24–27)

What is at once horrible and familiar about this declaration is its nauseating blend of legalism, sadism, and public relations, as if Cornwall were already thinking about how he will excuse the fact that there were certain regrettable excesses in his otherwise legal treatment of the prisoner.[7]

The plucking out of the Earl of Gloucester's eyes seems to have appalled even hardened Jacobean spectators, and the language of the play cunningly anticipates the act, so as to intensify its horror. This pattern of anticipations culminates in Gloucester's response to the repeated question, "Wherefore to Dover?" "Because I would not see thy cruel nails / Pluck out his poor old eyes" (3.7.56–58). Cornwall's response— "See 't shalt thou never" (3.7.68), he says, gouging out the first of the prisoner's eyes— provokes a reaction that may, for contemporary audiences, have been more shocking than the act of torture. A nameless servant steps forward and orders his master to stop what he is doing:

> Hold your hand, my lord:
> I have served you ever since I was a child;
> But better service have I never done you
> Than now to bid you hold. (3.7.73–76)

Regan's exclamation ("How now, you dog!") and Cornwall's ("My villain!") both reflect their astonishment at the source of the intervention: not one of Gloucester's servants (for they are, after all, in Gloucester's house) but one of their own (3.7.77, 81). In the ensuing scuffle, Regan grabs a sword and stabs the underling in the back—"A peasant stand up thus!" (3.7.83)—but not before the peasant has fatally wounded the duke. And the audience is manifestly invited to endorse this radical act: the murder of a ruler by a serving man who stands up for human decency.

Though his act has important political consequences, the servant is not acting out of party allegiance, and still less out of personal ambition. He has an ethically adequate object—the desire to serve the duke his master by stopping him at all costs from performing an unworthy action. He does not seek power for himself, nor is there anything to indicate that he supports the French invaders. His dying words to Gloucester—"My lord, you have one eye left / To see some mischief on him" (3.7.84–85)—suggest that in his last moments of life the servant has shifted his allegiance from Cornwall to Cornwall's victim, but this attempt at consolation only leads to further disaster. "Lest it see more," rages the mortally wounded Cornwall, turning back to Gloucester, "prevent it. Out, vile jelly!" (3.7.86).

In the folio text of *King Lear* the scene ends with Regan driving the eyeless earl out of his own house with words almost fantastic in their cruelty—"Go thrust him out at gates, and let him smell / His way to Dover" (3.7.96–97)—while the bleeding Cornwall disposes of the corpse of the servant: "Throw this slave / Upon the dunghill" (3.7.100–101). The quarto text has an additional brief exchange between two other nameless servants, who, like their slain fellow, have no large political agenda or ambition but express a fundamentally ethical attitude toward authority: "I'll never care what wickedness I do," says one, reflecting on Cornwall's action, "If this man come to good" (*History of King Lear*, scene 14, 96–97).

The ruler thus serves as an exemplar or test case: if his actions go unpunished, then, to paraphrase Dostoevsky, everything is permitted. The other servant is thinking not about the husband but about the wife:

> If she live long
> And in the end meet the old course of death,
> Women will all turn monsters.
> (*History of King Lear*, scene 14, 97–99)

Here again the ruler is a kind of test case, in this case for what it means to be human.

The servants' closing words turn from moral speculation to action. One of them proposes to find someone to lead the blinded earl wherever he wants to go; the other has a more immediate concern:

> I'll fetch some flax and whites of eggs
> To apply to his bleeding face.
> (*History of King Lear*, scene 14, 103–4)

In the bleak, stripped-down world of *King Lear*, this simple human response is itself potentially risky. Given the ruthlessness and fear of Cornwall and Regan, any gesture of kindness toward the traitor may be regarded as treasonous. Gloucester is anxious to avoid drawing anyone else into danger:

> Away, get thee away! Good friend, be gone.
> Thy comforts can do me no good at all;
> Thee they may hurt. (4.1.15–17)

But the quiet reply recognizes Gloucester's predicament—"you cannot see your way" (4.1.18)—and the human obligation to help him.

This fundamental ethical responsibility, reduced to the simplest elements—flax and egg whites applied to the victim's bleeding face—is echoed repeatedly in other moments of solidarity and comfort, all comparably modest: "Come on, my boy. How dost, my boy? Art cold?" (3.2.66). "Give me thy hand" (3.4.42). "In, fellow, there, into the hovel; keep thee warm" (3.4.162). These small gestures are the core of the play's moral vision. Larger ethical ambitions, such as those that motivate Cordelia's refusal to flatter her bullying father, only lead to disastrous consequences.

At the height of the storm scene, the crazed Lear, exposed to the tyranny of the elements, has a fleeting glimpse of a relationship to power different from the one he had embodied:

> Take physic, pomp;
> Expose thyself to feel what wretches feel,
> That thou mayst shake the superflux to them,
> And show the heavens more just. (3.4.34–37)

The vision of obligation here is modest enough—"shake the superflux" (that is, let some wealth trickle down to the wretches at the bottom)—but nothing in the play suggests that it is remotely possible to achieve. Lear lurches instead toward the conviction that there is no significant moral distinction between judges and thieves. "See how yond justice rails upon yond simple thief," he tells Gloucester; "Hark, in thine ear. Change places and, handy-dandy, which is the justice, which is the thief?" (4.6.147–49). All that secures the difference between them is a monopoly of violence. Have you ever "seen a farmer's dog bark at a beggar?" Lear asks. When you see the man running away from the cur, you behold "the great image of authority: a dog's obeyed in office" (4.5.150–53). Those in power may loudly declare their compassion for the sufferings of the poor, but inevitably the declarations are mere hypocrisy. "Get thee glass eyes," Lear says bitterly to the blind Gloucester,

> And, like a scurvy politician, seem
> To see the things thou dost not. (4.6.164–66)

Small wonder that the close of the play is a chorus of renunciation. With Cornwall, Regan, Goneril, Edmund, and Cordelia all dead, and Lear a crazed and broken ruin, the duke of Albany is the sole legitimate ruler of the kingdom, but he does not want it:

> For us, we will resign,
> During the life of this old majesty,
> To him our absolute power. (5.3.297–99)

A moment later Lear is dead, and Albany is still trying to give up his power. "Friends of my soul," he addresses Kent and Edgar,

> you twain
> Rule in this realm, and the gored state sustain. (5.3.318–19)

But neither will Kent have anything to do with rule:

> I have a journey, sir, shortly to go;
> My master calls me, I must not say no. (5.3.320–21)

The final lines of the play are a famous textual crux, for the quarto assigns them to Albany and the folio to Edgar. Since the last words of Elizabethan and Jacobean tragedies and histories were conventionally spoken by the person in command, the stakes are significant, but here, as none of the survivors wants power—as if any desire for power has been stigmatized as vicious—Shakespeare evidently was uncertain how to bring his tragedy to an end.

He had begun with a king who wished to withdraw from power and to reassure himself with comfortable falsehoods, public affirmations of his own limitless importance and value and generosity that he demanded of his children. In the course of the play those falsehoods are relentlessly stripped away, like the train of followers who had given the imperious Lear a sense of his own worth. But in the wake of the devastation, what is left? Shakespeare's solution was to end his great tragedy with an ambiguous, exceedingly reluctant accession to rule and then to turn the closing words away from any assumption of authority and toward the necessity, under immense pressure, of emotional honesty:

> The weight of this sad time we must obey;
> Speak what we feel, not what we ought to say. (5.3.322–23)

The dream of the absolute with which the play opens, whether absolute power or absolute love, has been destroyed forever. But the terrible sense of limit articulated at the close—the weight, the sadness of the time, the need to obey—has brought with it the strange injunction that is one of Shakespeare's most remarkable gifts, the simple injunction to speak what we feel.

CHAPTER FIVE

Shakespearean Autonomy

"Aesthetic autonomy," the will-o-the-wisp that haunted Theodor Adorno, was not a phrase that Shakespeare, who had a passion for rare expressions, could possibly have encountered.[1] If the *Oxford English Dictionary* is to be believed, "aesthetic"—which, as the term for a science or philosophy of taste, first emerged with Baumgarten's *Aesthetica* in the mid-eighteenth century—did not appear in English until the nineteenth century, and then only with many reservations. "There has lately grown into use in the arts," wrote the English architect Joseph Gwilt in 1842, "a silly pedantic term under the name of Æsthetics." It is, Gwilt added, "one of the metaphysical and useless additions to nomenclature in the arts in which the German writers abound."[2]

Shakespeare might, however, have recognized the word "autonomy." Though the first appearance in print recorded by the *Oxford English Dictionary* came seven years after Shakespeare's death, in fact it shows up in a work published in 1591 that must have been in limited circulation among intellectuals.[3] The book in which "autonomy" was first defined—Henry Cockeram's 1623 *The English dictionarie, or an interpreter of hard English words*—suggests that it was already in use, though only in the restricted sense of a "hard" word. It meant, as Cockeram puts it, "libertie to live after ones owne law."[4]

This definition was evidently meant to be more paradoxical than it now sounds, since in the early seventeenth century the word "liberty" had the distinct sense of a reckless freedom or licentiousness. "Never did I hear," Hotspur remarks of the disreputable tavern life of Prince Hal, "Of any prince so wild a liberty" (*1 Henry 4* 5.2.70–71), and Timon of Athens, cursing his ungrateful city, prays that "Lust and liberty" will

> Creep in the minds and marrows of our youth,
> That 'gainst the stream of virtue they may strive
> And drown themselves in riot! (4.1.25–28)

For a Jacobean reader, then, the phrase "liberty to live after one's own law" was something of a joke, since liberty and law were perpetually at war.

"Viva la libertà!" sings Don Giovanni, giving voice to the passionate anthem of one of the warring parties: it is tempting to follow the tracks of such liberty into libertinism, the erotic freedom that emerged in the Enlightenment as the shadow side of scientific rationality and the clearest consequence of the splintering of truth from beauty and beauty from goodness. From here it would only be a short step to the ironic vision of autonomy that opens Adorno's *Aesthetic Theory*, an autonomy that had begun as art's proud claim to absolute freedom and has ended in art's entrapment in a ceaseless, compulsive negation of its own origins or in art's degradation into cheap entertainment.

Shakespeare wrote for what was, in effect, a new and distinctly modern medium—a commercial, public theater, conspicuously detached from any ritual function. Not only were the London theaters, as physical structures, new to the urban setting—the first freestanding public theater in London dates from 1567—but the playing companies that performed in them profited from the deliberate Protestant strangulation of medieval theatrical rituals, rituals that had been too closely linked to the festive calendar of the outlawed Catholic Church.

The theater, as an enterprise, was risky, vulgar, unstable, and profane, and anyone involved in it was, as Shakespeare under-

stood perfectly well, socially and morally tainted. "Alas, 'tis true,"
he writes in sonnet 110,

> I have gone here and there
> And made myself a motley to the view,
> Gored mine own thoughts, sold cheap what is most dear.

This is the voice of someone who worked in the entertainment
business and knew the contempt heaped upon it. To make oneself "a motley to the view" is to become a clown, a huckster, a
throwaway figure of cheap, meaningless amusement.

No one with any self-respect would actively embrace such
a life; it was, like prostitution, a fate that befell you because of
circumstances, specifically, poverty. "O, for my sake do you with
fortune chide," Shakespeare pleads in sonnet 111,

> The guilty goddess of my harmful deeds,
> That did not better for my life provide
> Than public means which public manners breeds.

To appear as an entertainer before the public—not a chosen few
but a random mass of anonymous consumers who have the right
to whistle and laugh and shout at you because they have paid a
penny at the door—is to be stained:

> Thence comes it that my name receives a brand,
> And almost thence my nature is subdued
> To what it works in, like the dyer's hand.

"Shakespeare" became in the playwright's own lifetime what we
would call a brand name—it could be invoked in advertisements
to get the crowds to part with their money, and it was sufficiently
marketable to be assigned fraudulently to plays he had certainly
not written—but this success was, or so he writes, like having his
name receive a brand. The image is of those convicted criminals

who were branded, usually on the hand, so that they would carry for the rest of their lives the indelible sign of their disgrace.

The sign was real enough for the York herald Ralph Brooke to file a formal complaint in 1602, objecting to the granting of a coat of arms, and hence the status of gentleman, to "Shakespeare ye Player." A player was by definition not a gentleman; he was someone who had commodified his identity. And indeed, even when the folio edition of Shakespeare's plays was produced, seven years after his death, the editors continued to present his achievement as a commodity, albeit a very expensive one. Alongside the obsequious dedicatory epistle to the Earl of Pembroke and the Earl of Montgomery, the editors, Shakespeare's friends John Heminges and Henry Condell, added a letter to "the great Variety of Readers," who ranged, as they put it, "from the most able, to him that can but spell." Heminges and Condell made clear what they wanted first and foremost from this amorphous group: "Whatever you do, buy." Complete the cash transaction. Then and only then would the purchasers be at liberty to set themselves up in judgment of the author—bearing in mind, however, that the plays they were encountering had already stood trial in the public theater and emerged unscathed. "Read him, therefore; and again, and again," the editors write. "And if then you do not like him, surely you are in some manifest danger, not to understand him."⁵

Understanding and hence liking Shakespeare, as Heminges and Condell conceive it, has nothing at all to do with moral high-mindedness, with any imaginable school curriculum, or with what the sociologist Pierre Bourdieu calls "cultural capital." Early seventeenth-century plays in the vernacular by modern playwrights had no such capital. In 1612 Thomas Bodley instructed the first keeper of his library in Oxford to exclude from the shelves "such books as almanacs, plays, and an infinite number, that are daily printed, of very unworthy matters." "Baggage books," he called them.⁶ Bodley was evidently not alone: though an estimated 750 copies were printed and the edition sold out in less than a decade, an exhaustive census has turned up only a single early reference to the First Folio in any library catalog or donors' inventory.

Shakespeare's texts, then, were brought into the literary marketplace under the sign not of obligation, duty, self-improvement, academic prestige, or aesthetic seriousness but of pleasure.

Shakespeare himself evidently gave some consideration to a socially respectable form of artistic ambition, one that did not carry the stigma of public means and public manners. During what must have been a very difficult period in the mid-1590s, when a particularly virulent and extended outbreak of bubonic plague led the authorities to shut down all of the theaters, he turned his attention to the familiar and traditional way in which artists could receive financial support without incurring disgrace: patronage. He wrote two splendid mythological poems, *Venus and Adonis* and *The Rape of Lucrece*, both elegantly printed by his friend Nathan Field and both lovingly dedicated to the enormously wealthy young aristocrat Henry Wriothesley, third Earl of Southampton.

Shakespeare's strategy may have succeeded—his poems were hugely popular among the elite at Oxford and Cambridge, and he was rumored to have received a startlingly large sum as a gift from the young earl. But as soon as the plague deaths abated and the theaters were allowed to reopen, Shakespeare evidently returned to his disreputable vocation. Indeed, he may have used whatever money the earl had given him to buy a share in the playing company, becoming literally invested in the entertainment business, a business lodged not in an aristocratic household, let alone a sacred precinct, but in a vulgar arena open to all.

This exposure to the masses was, Shakespeare understood, diametrically opposed to the privacy that had been the traditional privilege, or at least the fantasy, of the aristocracy. But he saw the emergence of a peculiar link between the actor and the new rulers of the centralized state. Those rulers—who were, for reasons of personal entertainment and prestige, the patrons and protectors of the theater companies—were themselves drawn (or compelled) to acts of theatrical self-display. In *Julius Caesar* the aristocratic Casca expresses his disgust that Caesar's ambition has led him to perform a charade before the crowd:

> the rabblement hooted, and clapped their chapped hands, and threw up their sweaty nightcaps, and uttered such a deal of stinking breath because Caesar refused the crown that it had almost choked Caesar; for he swooned and fell down at it. (1.2.243–46)

The hooting, clapping, and cheering that provoked this comical catastrophe were, of course, precisely what Shakespeare and his fellow actors were in the business of evoking. Politicians—a word with sharply negative connotations in this period—could do the same, but a true aristocrat would despise such public exposure. So intense is the aversion that surges up in Cleopatra, when she contemplates being displayed to the "shouting varletry" of Rome, that she prefers death to what she knows lies in store for her in captivity:

> Saucy lictors
> Will catch at us like strumpets, and scald rhymers
> Ballad us out o' tune. The quick comedians
> Extemporally will stage us, and present
> Our Alexandrian revels. Antony
> Shall be brought drunken forth, and I shall see
> Some squeaking Cleopatra boy my greatness
> I'th' posture of a whore.
> (*Antony and Cleopatra* 5.2.55, 5.2.210–17)

Cleopatra is here contemplating being displayed and mocked as an abject captive; elsewhere she is hardly averse to spectacular and highly public performances of herself. But those are performances she can employ to assert her status, her power, and her royal line. Caesar in disgust shares with his friends reports that

have reached him about the theatrical goings-on in which Antony has participated in Alexandria:

> I'th' market place on a tribunal silvered,
> Cleopatra and himself in chairs of gold
> Were publicly enthroned. At the feet sat
> Caesarion, whom they call my father's son,
> And all the unlawful issue that their lust
> Since then hath made between them. Unto her
> He gave the stablishment of Egypt; made her
> Of lower Syria, Cyprus, Lydia,
> Absolute queen. (3.6.3–11)

To Maecenas's incredulous question, "This in the public eye?"
Caesar replies, insisting on the literal theatricality of it all: "I'th'
common showplace, where they exercise" (3.6.11–12).

Cleopatra chooses the "common showplace" as the stage on
which to dress up in order to make her most extravagant performance, her apotheosis:

> She
> In th'habiliments of the goddess Isis
> That day appeared. (3.6.16–18)

This masquerade, as Shakespeare's audience would have understood, was not (or not only) an exercise in mad vanity; the identification with divinity was part of what it meant to claim to be
an "absolute queen." English monarchs did not routinely dress up
as gods and goddesses (apart from the theatrical rituals known as
masques); but Elizabeth and James both assumed the mantle of
divine authority, God's absolute liberty to live after his own law.

That the concept of autonomy evidently emerged in this period as more than a mere paradox is probably linked to the highly
explicit and insistent claim made by James I for his right to rule
above the law as well as under the law of the realm. Kings, wrote

James in *The Trew Law of Free Monarchies*, are "the authors and makers of the Lawes, and not the Lawes of the kings." Power does not derive from the people, nor is an authentic king's rule in any way conditional: "power flowes always from him selfe," James declared, for "the King is aboue the law."[7] Of course, he acknowledged, a good king will ordinarily frame his actions according to the law, to set an example for his subjects, but he is not bound to do so, for he himself is in no way a subject.

The king's position was by no means uncontested: Holinshed's *Chronicles*, to cite Shakespeare's favorite source for English history, stated flatly that Parliament held "the most high and absolute power of the realm, for thereby kings and mighty princes have from time to time been deposed from their thrones."[8] But James's assertion of royal autonomy had already been made in the reign of his predecessor, Elizabeth I, by the crown lawyers, who based their arguments on venerable legal and philosophical theories of princely power that extended back through the Middle Ages to ancient Roman jurisprudence. In the thirteenth century Frederick II's *Liber augustalis* asserted that the Caesar "must be at once the *Father and Son of Justice* [*pater et filius Iustitiae*]," a status explicitly linked to the law (the *lex regia*) by which the Quirites conferred the *imperium* on the Roman *princeps*.[9] That power included both a limited right to create law and an exemption from the law, an exemption that had an obvious appeal to any monarch with absolutist pretensions.

One may glimpse this appeal in Shakespeare where one might least expect it: in the comedies.[10] There a ruler repeatedly finds himself initially constrained by law to do something against his will and pleasure. Thus, for example, in *The Comedy of Errors*, Duke Solinus is apparently obliged to enforce upon the Syracusan merchant Egeon what "hath in solemn synods been decreed," namely:

> if any Syracusian born
> Come to the bay of Ephesus—he dies,

His goods confiscate to the Duke's dispose,
Unless a thousand marks be levièd
To quit the penalty and ransom him. (1.1.13, 18–22)

When he learns why the unfortunate merchant has ventured to
come to Ephesus—to search for his missing son—Solinus does
not wish to carry out the stern decree, but he has no choice:

Now trust me, were it not against our laws—
Which princes, would they, may not disannul—
Against my crown, my oath, my dignity,
My soul should sue as advocate for thee. (1.1.142–45)

"My crown, my oath, my dignity"—the language here is explicitly monarchic, the crown being the emblem of royal sovereignty,
the oath of royal coronation, and the dignity of royal continuity
and perpetuity. As a kind individual, Solinus sympathizes with
the unfortunate man, condemned to die, but as a ruler he can do
nothing to avert the execution: "we may pity though not pardon
thee" (1.1.97).

And yet, of course, at the end of *The Comedy of Errors* the
merchant is not executed; he is reunited not only with the son
for whom he was searching but also with his long-lost wife and
with his son's twin brother, both of whom he had presumed dead.
That twin, a wealthy man, steps forward with a full purse to ransom his father, according to the law that the duke had so clearly
articulated in the play's first scene.

This ransom would have been a perfect climactic comic device, since the audience has been carefully led to follow the purse,
from the moment when the wealthy twin, under arrest for debt,
sends his servant with a key to fetch it from "the desk /That's
covered o'er with Turkish tapestry" (4.1.103–4) to the moment
when it is delivered by the servant to the wrong twin to the
moment when it is returned to its rightful owner. But, having
shown the audience precisely what he could so easily have done,

Shakespeare chooses not to do it. Instead, when offered the legal ransom for the condemned prisoner, the duke peremptorily refuses it:

ANTIPHOLUS OF EPHESUS These ducats pawn I for my father
    here.
DUKE It shall not need. Thy father hath his life. (5.1.391–92)

So much for the law.

Shakespeare repeats what is essentially the same scheme in *A Midsummer Night's Dream*. There Egeus, outraged that his daughter Hermia has refused to marry the man he has chosen for her, comes before Duke Theseus with a formal complaint:

I beg the ancient privilege of Athens:
As she is mine, I may dispose of her,
Which shall be either to this gentleman
Or to her death, according to our law
Immediately provided in that case. (1.1.41–45)

When Hermia requests legal clarification—"that I may know / The worst that may befall me in this case" (1.1.62–63)—she is told that she faces either execution or life in a nunnery. Theseus urges her to reconsider:

        look you arm yourself
To fit your fancies to your father's will,
Or else the law of Athens yields you up—
Which by no means we may extenuate—
To death or to a vow of single life. (1.1.117–21)

The succession of mad events—the flight to the moonlit woods, the encounter with the fairies, the tangle of confusions—follows directly from Theseus's inability to "extenuate" the harsh law of Athens. Yet here too the plot is resolved in the end simply by fiat. "Enough, enough, my lord, you have enough. / I beg the law," sputters the irate father, when he finds his wayward daughter in the arms of the man with whom she has eloped. But Duke Theseus brushes the demand away in a single line: "Egeus, I will overbear your will" (4.1.151–52, 176).

What Shakespeare seems to be staging is not simply the triumph of kinship, at the end of *The Comedy of Errors*, and the triumph of love, at the end of *A Midsummer Night's Dream*, but the triumph of the prince over the law. But this princely triumph is not a principled one. No one proclaims the liberation of the royal crown, the oath, and the dignity from the constraints of the law on which they have been said to depend. On the contrary, the rulers in both of the plays seem simply to forget about the clear, inflexible norms they had earlier declared themselves powerless to alter. If the comic release depends upon the ruler's autonomy, it is evidently an autonomy that dare not speak its name. Or rather it finds its voice only in the accents of comedy's gratuitous transformation of fear into pleasure.

Most of Shakespeare's kings make at least a show of being bound by law and custom. The conniving Richard III stages an elaborate charade in which the "citizens" supposedly appeal to him to accept the crown. "O make them joyful," entreats his cynical sidekick Catesby, "grant their lawful suit" (3.7.193). Claudius, Hamlet complains bitterly, has "Popped in between th'election and my hopes" (5.2.66), but that means that an election brought the murderer to the throne. And even bloodstained Macbeth is formally invested, as if he were the most law-abiding of men, with the sovereignty he has in fact ruthlessly seized.

There are rulers in Shakespeare who formally attempt to act as if they were above the law—Richard II, for example, or King Lear—but they are for this reason immediately entangled in the disaster that Ernst Kantorowicz famously called "the tragedy of the King's Two Bodies."[11] The theological and political implications of this tragedy, so richly explored by Kantorowicz and by those who have followed in his broad wake, are not directly relevant to the question of whether aesthetic autonomy has any meaning for Shakespeare. To answer that question we need to know, first, whether Shakespeare could even have conceived of autonomy as a concept, independent of the catastrophic behavior of his tragic kings, and, second, whether he could have applied this concept to works of art or to the artists who fashioned them.

If Shakespeare staged something like the happy affirmation of autonomy in the two comedies we have discussed, the happiness of the affirmation seems to depend on simply forgetting the constraints of the law rather than formally negating them. No special right is proclaimed, no concept of sovereignty articulated. In actual social practice, as Shakespeare understood, the unspoken may be more eloquent than the spoken, and the order of things that asserts itself spontaneously—as the apparently improvisational expression of a collective desire—may be more powerful than the official rule painstakingly promulgated and theoretically defended.

But there is evidence that autonomy as a concept interested Shakespeare, even if the word itself remained unfamiliar to him. He reflected repeatedly in his plays on at least three different ways in which one might be at liberty to live after one's own law. There is a dream of physical autonomy, exemption from the mortal vulnerability of the flesh or at least from the fear this vulnerability instinctively arouses. There is a recurrent dream of social autonomy, independence from the dense network of friends, family, and alliances that ties the individual to a carefully ordered world. And there is a dream of mental autonomy, the ability to dwell in a separate psychic world, a heterocosm of one's own making.

The three dreams are conjoined on at least one occasion, in Shakespeare's depiction of Coriolanus, the military savior of Rome and then, in exile, the leader of Rome's Volscian enemies. Coriolanus is not in any literal sense physically invulnerable; on the contrary, his flesh bears many scars from a life of military combat (twenty-seven of them, by his mother's count, well before the play has reached the halfway point). But it is as if he were exempt from the terror, pain, suffering, and lingering infection that afflict all other mortals whose skin is breached again and again by sharp steel. He speaks dismissively of his "unaching scars" (2.2.145) and is repeatedly described by others as a being who is not fully human, indeed, not fully a living creature at all:

> As weeds before
> A vessel under sail, so men obeyed
> And fell below his stem. His sword, death's stamp,
> Where it did mark, it took. From face to foot
> He was a thing of blood, whose every motion
> Was timed with dying cries. Alone he entered
> The mortal gate of th' city, which he, painted
> With shunless destiny, aidless came off,
> And with a sudden reinforcement struck
> Corioles like a planet. (2.2.101–10)

The laws that govern the lives of others do not govern Coriolanus. He seems to have willed himself outside them, just as he wills himself outside the social laws that regulate everyone else, from the proudest aristocrat to the humblest artificer, in the polis. The polities of the ancient world fascinated Shakespeare precisely because they enabled him to think outside a monarchical system in which all power flowed (or at least was said to flow) from the king. Rome has no king, and it is Coriolanus's proud refusal to participate in the popular rites of power—specifically, the humble soliciting of votes and hence the acknowledgment of dependency—that has led to his exile.

Nothing seems to be left of the ties that once bound Coriolanus to his countrymen. "You have," the Volscian general Aufidius says to him,

> stopped your ears against
> The general suit of Rome. (5.3.5–6)

Aufidius has every reason to doubt his former enemy's loyalty to the interests of the Volsces, but he acknowledges that Coriolanus has made himself deaf to the collective claims — the "general suit" — of the community to which he once belonged. That community has branded him an "enemy to the people and his country," and Coriolanus for his part has transformed banishment into a declaration of independence: "I banish you" (3.3.122, 127). He has proclaimed that the laws of the city no longer apply to him: this is, as Shakespeare conceived it, the necessary first step toward autonomy. "I go alone," Coriolanus tells his mother as he leaves the city:

> Like to a lonely dragon that his fen
> Makes feared and talked of more than seen. (4.1.30–32)

Shakespeare repeatedly made use of false endings, moments the action of a play seems to reach a conclusion, as happens here, only to lurch forward again. Rome cannot stomach Coriolanus, however important he has been to the city as a virtually unstoppable war machine, and it has driven him out. He walks through the city gates into a mythical space, as he imagines it, and assumes an identity that no longer conforms to human shape. His participation in the human community is finished.

This rupture is a conceivable ending to the tragedy, but of course it is not the ending that Shakespeare chose. For a vision of radical independence — that is, of autonomy — depends precisely on a continuing relationship that is continually denied. If the relationship is simply broken, completely and finally, if Coriolanus is never seen or heard from again, if he becomes a mythical creature, his destiny would be a vanishing rather than an instance of "liberty to live after one's own law."

Hence the necessity, theoretical as well as theatrical, of the exiled hero's appearance once more at the gates of the city, now not as its defender but as its implacable enemy, the embodiment of murderous negation. Hence too his stopping of his ears against the general suit of Rome. To stop one's ears is still to hear, however much the sound is muted; what is required is the will not to listen. This is why Aufidius is not being absurd when he expresses admiration for Coriolanus's ability to keep from registering what is in fact reaching his senses: not only the wailings of the frightened city but also its whispered pleas. It is more difficult, he understands, to block still, small voices, with their intimate claims, than clamorous appeals. Coriolanus, the Volscian acknowledges, has

> never admitted
> A private whisper, no, not with such friends
> That thought them sure of you. (5.3.6–8)

"Mine ears against your suits are stronger than / Your gates against my force" (5.2.84–85), Coriolanus grimly tells one of these friends, the weeping old man, Menenius Agrippa, whom he once called father.

For Shakespeare the state of being that Coriolanus wishes to enter (the state of being we would now call autonomy) only begins when he frees himself from the laws of the polis; the private whispers — the innumerable secret ways in which the world shapes any life — are the more difficult challenge. A moment later a new group of supplicants arrives, including Coriolanus's wife Virgilia, his young son Martius, and, above all, his formidable mother Volumnia. Once again he remains unmoved. The intimate claims made upon him by wife, son, and mother are forms of dependence, and hence of heteronomy, that he decisively rejects. And in rejecting these claims, he articulates what is for him — and perhaps for his creator, Shakespeare — the heart of the matter:

> I'll never
> Be such a gosling to obey instinct, but stand
> As if a man were author of himself
> And knew no other kin. (5.3.34–37)

"As if a man were author of himself": self-authorship must for Coriolanus be the defining feature of his identity, the core of his sense of uniqueness and self-worth. He refuses to recognize biological and psychological entailments, just as he refuses to bend to the desperate social, economic, and political appeals directed at him. Only by severing his relationship to nature and abstracting himself from all claims of kinship, will he become absolutely autonomous.

And then suddenly, when his mother kneels before him, Coriolanus collapses:

> O mother, mother!
> What have you done? (5.3.183–84)

The suddenness of the collapse—like a dam bursting—suggests how much weight in the phrase "as if a man were author of himself" was being borne by the words "as if." There was a creature—the phoenix—that, as Lactantius wrote, "is son to himself, is his own father, and his own heir,"[12] but Coriolanus turns out to be far more a gosling than a phoenix.

Autonomy is his cherished fantasy of dignity and freedom, but it is untrue both to the psychic bonds that were forged at his birth and to the social bonds that were forged by the community that gave him his honorific name. For that matter it is untrue to the person he is just before the moment of his collapse, for at that moment he is not in fact utterly independent. To be sure, he no longer serves and thus represents the community of his birth, but he represents a different community: "My affairs," he has told Menenius, "Are servanted to others" (5.2.78–79). Thus Coriolanus understands very well that his mother's triumphant claim is likely to mean his death—

> for your son, believe it, O believe it,
> Most dangerously you have with him prevailed,
> If not most mortal to him—

and he understands too that he cannot avert his fate: "But let it come" (5.3.188–90).

When his fate does come, a very short time later, it is wrapped in the language of the relationships that shaped him long before he came into the hard, implacable manhood he so prizes. Aufidius, who has been plotting his murder, contemptuously calls him "boy"—"thou boy of tears" (5.6.103)—and the word, triggering in Coriolanus an infantile burst of rage, drives him to remind the Volsces of all the mayhem and misery he has brought them over the years. The crowd around him erupts:

> Tear him to pieces! Do it presently!
> He killed my son! My daughter! He killed my cousin
> Marcus! He killed my father! (5.6.121–23)

The last words to reach Coriolanus's ears are society's definitive response to the man who imagines that he can live after his own law: "Kill, kill, kill, kill, kill him!" (5.6.130).

Coriolanus suggests that, though he was fascinated by the idea of autonomy, Shakespeare doubted that it was possible even for the most fiercely determined human being to live as if he were the author of himself. Autonomy in the strict sense is not a state available for any sentient creature. Warriors may persuade themselves that they are singularly free, just as kings may be flattered by their followers into believing that they are absolute, but the reality is always otherwise. "You have but mistook me all this while," the downcast Richard II tells his friends:

> I live with bread, like you; feel want,
> Taste grief, need friends. Subjected thus,
> How can you say to me I am a king? (*Richard 2* 3.2.170–73)

So too Lear learns to his grief that he is "subjected." His position had fostered in him the illusion that the world would always conform to his will—"To say 'aye' and 'no' to everything that I said!"—but the relentless stripping away of his power discloses the vulnerable, shivering mortal beneath the robes of office:

> When the rain came to wet me once, and the wind to make me chatter; when the thunder would not peace at my bidding; there I found 'em, there I smelt 'em out. Go to, they are not men o' their words! They told me I was everything. 'Tis a lie, I am not ague-proof. (4.6.97–103)

Ague—the flu—is the zero-degree challenge to the dream of autonomy, bleak proof that "unaccommodated man," as Lear puts it to the mad beggar, "is no more but such a poor, bare, forked animal as thou art" (3.4.98–100).

But if some form of subjection is the inescapable human condition, Shakespeare may nonetheless have thought that radical freedom was possible for a made object, that is, for a poem or a play. He may have thought too that such freedom was possible for the artist in the act of making those objects. After all, he perfectly grasped the difference, fully theorized in his time, between a particular, all-too-human king and a royal effigy, such as the lifelike one of Henry VII that may still be viewed in Westminster Abbey. The former was not ague-proof, but the latter, a *persona ficta*, represented the royal Dignity that never died. Shakespeare's great contemporary, the jurist Sir Edward Coke, observed that the mortal king was God-made, but the immortal King, man-made.[13]

Shakespeare's sonnets to the young man, promising him symbolic immortality, are predicated on this traditional distinction, though it is one that Shakespeare made characteristically his own by intensifying the sense of paradoxicality:

> Since brass, nor stone, nor earth, nor boundless sea,
> But sad mortality o'ersways their power,
> How with this rage shall beauty hold a plea,
> Whose action is no stronger than a flower? (Sonnet 65)

Here it is not only flesh and blood that are subject to the ravages of time—figured as an oppressive, unstoppable military force—but also brass and stone, the materials out of which effigies themselves are fashioned. Nothing and no one escapes from a subjection to which the earth and sea themselves are bound, as the last lines of the sonnet put it,

> unless this miracle have might:
> That in black ink my love may still shine bright.

The miracle—and it is one that is carefully hedged about with doubt—would be the miracle of aesthetic autonomy: the exemption of an aesthetic object from the laws that govern all other material objects.

The aesthetic object in question is itself a material object: it is made of black ink. Hence the special force of the miracle, for of all substances black ink is the least likely to transmit bright shining beauty. Shakespeare plays repeatedly with this paradox, whose power depends on what Adorno famously called "negativity":

> His beauty shall in these black lines be seen,
> And they shall live, and he in them still green. (Sonnet 63)

It is by virtue not of mimetic likeness but of negation that Shakespeare's poems lay claim to the special status of enduring works of art.

As we have seen, negation extends in Shakespeare beyond the witty play on the blackness of ink—a miraculous exemption from the decay to which everything else is bound—to both a profound critique of the norms of beauty and an exploration of the limits of hatred. But perhaps, from the perspective of aesthetic autonomy, what matters is less the precise object of negation than the dream of the miracle itself. Shakespeare did not need the whole philosophical apparatus that surrounded aesthetics in the eighteenth century to imagine the claim that the literary artist was at liberty to live after his own law and that his creations were singularly free and unconstrained. And he did not need simply to intuit this claim. He had the example of his contemporary Christopher Marlowe, who wrote as if there were no constraints on his will to absolute play.[14] He had also at his disposal an account of artistic freedom, with conceptual roots in Plato and Aristotle, that was affirmed by a number of Renaissance literary theorists and received a powerful articulation in the early 1580s in Sir Philip Sidney's *Apology for Poetry*.

Sidney acknowledged that human art in general cannot stand alone. "There is no art delivered to mankind that hath not the works of nature for his principal object," he wrote, "without which they could not consist, and on which they so depend, as they become actors and players, as it were, of what nature will have set forth."[15] To be an actor or player was, for the aristocratic Sidney, the antithesis of autonomy, the epitome of an absolute dependence on the commands of another. Such dependence is, he went on to say, the inescapable, defining condition of the astronomer, the geometrician, the arithmetician, the musician, the natural and moral philosopher, the lawyer, the grammarian, rhetorician, and logician, the physician and the metaphysician. Sidney prudently sets aside one profession from this list of those who must observe the rules set by a higher power: the "Divine" or cleric, he writes, is "with all reverence . . . ever to be excepted."[16] But, of course, the divine is more than anyone else subjected to an absolute authority—not the authority of nature but that of nature's creator. There is but a single genuine exception to the principle of subordination:

> Only the poet, disdaining to be tied to any such subjection, lifted up with the vigor of his own invention, doth grow in effect another nature, in making things either better than nature bringeth forth, or quite anew, forms such as never were in nature, as the Heroes, Demigods, Cyclops, Chimeras, Furies, and such like; so as he goeth hand in hand with nature, not enclosed within the

narrow warrant of her gifts, but freely ranging only within the zodiac of his own wit.

Unique among artists, the poet refuses any dependence upon nature, a dependence that he regards as a form of "subjection."

Sidney knew from painful experience what it was to be the subject of a powerful queen—his bridling against subjection was one of the recurrent themes of his life, and his great works, *Astrophil and Stella* and *Arcadia,* are complex meditations on boundaries and constraints. But in *The Apology for Poetry*, he acted out his aristocratic disdain and rose up against the bondage. His language is not quite that of outright rebellion, but it is something more than a mere escape from an unwelcome tie. For once the link to nature is broken, as Sidney claimed it is in the greatest poetry, anything is possible. The biological laws of generation—whose psychic force overwhelms Coriolanus in the presence of his mother—are overturned: hence the symbolic force of the chimera, with its lion's head, goat's body, and serpent's tail.

Certain poets—Sidney's examples include Lucretius and the Virgil of the *Georgics*—accept the laws of nature and the limitations that these laws entail. "It must not be imagined," Lucretius wrote, "that all kinds of atoms can be linked together in all kinds of combinations; otherwise you would witness the creation of prodigious things everywhere: monsters, half-human, half-brute, would appear; sometimes tall branches would sprout from the trunk of a living creature; often the limbs of terrestrial and marine animals would be united; and Chimaeras, belching flame from their hellish throats, would be nourished by nature throughout the all-producing earth."[17] Of course, as Lucretius knew very well, to say that these things must not be imagined is at the same time to imagine them, but the point is to understand, as he put it, that "none of these things happens." For Sidney, though, such a servile submission to the laws of nature calls into question whether writers like Lucretius, writers whose work "is wrapped within the fold of the proposed subject, and takes

not the course of his own invention," should even be called poets. "Whether they properly be poets or no let grammarians dis-
pute," he dismissively remarks, turning his attention to those
whom he calls "right poets." The difference, he explains,

> is such a kind of difference as betwixt the meaner sort of paint-
> ers, who counterfeit only such faces as are set before them, and
> the more excellent, who having no law but wit, bestow that in
> colours upon you which is fittest for the eye to see.[18]

"Having no law but wit": while servile artists are mere counter-
feiters, chained to the world, the "more excellent" painters, like
the more excellent poets, are autonomous.

Sidney, whose portrait was painted by Veronese, thought that
even the most excellent painter practiced something he termed
"imitation," that is, mimetic representation. But the best artists,
in his view, "to imitate borrow nothing of what is, hath been, or
shall be; but range, only reined with learned discretion, into the
divine consideration of what may be and should be." It is difficult to grasp exactly what it could mean for the painter of a portrait to "borrow nothing of what is"; perhaps in such a case the
phrase would designate only an idealized likeness of the kind
that Sidney—whose face, according to Ben Jonson, was "spoiled
with pimples"—may have preferred. The example Sidney himself gave is not a portrait but a painting of the dying Lucretia,
"wherein he [the artist] painteth not Lucretia whom he never
saw, but painteth the outward beauty of such a virtue."

Sidney's insistence here on virtue is the key to his conception
of the poet's freedom. To be liberated from nature is to achieve
a moral clarity that actual circumstances tend to obscure, just as
the features of a particular face may obscure the virtue within.
Indeed, Sidney wrote, the fact that poetry can bring forth ideal
images that exceed anything that can be found in nature provides evidence for the fallenness of the human condition, "since
our erected wit maketh us know what perfection is, and yet our

infected will keepeth us from reaching unto it."[19] Poetic autonomy, then, in its capacity to abstract and idealize, keeps alive the
dream of a return to paradisal wholeness. Only by leaving the
world behind, only by freely ranging within the zodiac of his own
wit, can the poet lead himself and his readers toward redemption.

That Shakespeare knew this remarkable passage—or at the
very least knew the ideas that underlay it—is suggested by its
striking echoes throughout his work, perhaps above all in *A Midsummer Night's Dream*:

> The poet's eye, in a fine frenzy rolling,
> Doth glance from heaven to earth, from earth to heaven,
> And as imagination bodies forth
> The forms of things unknown, the poet's pen
> Turns them to shapes, and gives to airy nothing
> A local habitation and a name. (5.1.12–17)

These richly suggestive lines seem to imply some of the key ideas
that would later be explored under the rubric of aesthetic autonomy: that the work of art possesses a life of its own, independent
of the imperatives of the natural order of things; that the artist
is guided by a distinctive form of perception; that aesthetic experience is detached from everyday practical affairs and utilitar-
ian considerations; that the objects created by artists cannot be
known or judged in scientific or philosophical terms; that art is
a sphere of radical freedom.

This freedom, in Shakespeare's vision as in Sidney's, is linked
to an escape from the obligation to represent the world as it is,
an escape from nature. For Sidney, as we have seen, it was also
an escape from conceiving oneself as an actor or player. But for
Shakespeare, who was himself a player as well as a playwright,
there is virtually nothing of the redemptive hope, the exalted
moral vision, or the thinly concealed political aims that moti-
vated Sidney's account, nor is there anything of Sidney's aristocratic pride.[20] On the contrary, the lines I have quoted are part

of a speech in which Duke Theseus, hearing the lovers' account of their mad night in the Athenian woods, expresses his skepticism. "The lunatic, the lover, and the poet," he says with genial contempt, "Are of imagination all compact" (5.1.7–8). That is, they are linked by their "seething brains" and "shaping fantasies" (5.1.4–5). None of them perceives what is actually out there:

> One sees more devils than vast hell can hold:
> That is the madman. The lover, all as frantic,
> Sees Helen's beauty in a brow of Egypt. (5.1.9–11)

Under the influence of the imagination, the madman makes the world darker than it is, while the lover does not see the darkness that is before his eyes. In this company, the poet's ability to body forth the forms of things unknown is not the sign of the erected wit but of derangement, a tendency to distort reality either in the direction of irrational longing or of irrational fear:

> Such tricks hath strong imagination
> That if it would but apprehend some joy
> It comprehends some bringer of that joy;
> Or in the night, imagining some fear,
> How easy is a bush supposed a bear! (5.1.18–22)

It could be said, of course, that Theseus is the one who is deluded. Overly confident in his grasp of everyday reality, he fails to understand that the events the lovers describe, their mad, confused wanderings driven by the fairies' tricks, are precisely what the play depicts as actual. The actual is far more like a dream than those who claim to see everything clearly and distinctly can possibly imagine. Hence the ridiculous Bottom is closer to the truth in his jumbled recollection than the clear-eyed Theseus:

> I have had a most rare vision. I have had a dream past the wit of
> man to say what dream it was. Man is but an ass if he go about

t'expound this dream. Methought I was—there is no man can tell what. Methought I was, and methought I had—but man is but a patched fool if he will offer to say what methought I had. The eye of man hath not heard, the ear of man hath not seen, man's hand is not able to taste, his tongue to conceive, nor his heart to report what my dream was. (4.1.199–207)

This vision of the indescribable, the uninterpretable, the inconceivable—a parody of the first epistle to Corinthians, spoken by an exuberant, conceited ass who wants to play every part—is the moment in Shakespeare's theatrical works in which he comes closest to the idea of aesthetic autonomy. It is an idea suitable, Bottom thinks, to be presented to the ruler in a public performance: "I will get Peter Quince to write a ballad of this dream. It shall be called 'Bottom's Dream', because it hath no bottom, and I will sing it in the latter end of a play, before the Duke" (4.1.207–10).

We do not in fact hear Bottom's Dream at the end of the hilariously inept play that the mechanicals perform for the duke. Bottom offers to deliver an epilogue—perhaps the ballad he had hoped to sing—but the duke rejects it: "No epilogue, I pray you; for your play needs no excuse. Never excuse" (5.1.340–41). But *A Midsummer Night's Dream* does end with an exculpatory epilogue, of precisely the kind that the duke had summarily refused. Puck steps forward and discloses in effect that the entire play has been a bottomless dream:

> If we shadows have offended,
> Think but this, and all is mended:
> That you have but slumbered here,
> While these visions did appear;
> And this weak and idle theme,
> No more yielding but a dream,
> Gentles, do not reprehend.
> If you pardon, we will mend. (Epilogue 1–8)

If this is the play's summary claim to aesthetic autonomy, it is one that collapses Sidney's proud vision of the liberated imagination into something far more modest and more practical. The work of art lives after its own laws, in the way that a dream lives after its own laws.

The crucial point is that there is no reason to take offense, no reason, that is, to call the police. The players and the playwright know that their art is potentially vulnerable. They understand the specter of which Shakespeare complains in sonnet 66, when he bewails "art made tongue-tied by authority."[21] The artist's freedom depends upon a social agreement, a willingness on the part of the elite—the "gentles"—to permit it to exist and to exist without crushing, constant interference. Such a social agreement could, of course, easily entail the opposite of aesthetic autonomy: the artists might be led to acknowledge formally their direct dependence on their social superiors. The liberty of the artist, insofar as it exists at all, would consist entirely in an active willingness to submit, for it is only in submission, whether to artistic conventions or to social norms, that an artist acquires a voice that can be heard. And that voice consequently declares, both implicitly and explicitly, its determination never willingly to give offense.

This determination is what the blundering artisans attempt to articulate at the beginning of "Pyramus and Thisbe":

> If we offend, it is with our good will.
> That you should think: we come not to offend
> But with good will. To show our simple skill,
> That is the true beginning of our end. (5.1.108–11)

But Peter Quince's difficulties with punctuation make the attempt a disastrous failure—perhaps all such attempts are doomed to failure—and *A Midsummer Night's Dream* proposes in effect the terms of a different understanding: art has no more relation to reality than a dream does. It is at liberty to live after its own law, but only because it floats free of all practical significance. Its claim to meaninglessness, inconsequentiality, and idleness—"No more yielding but a dream"—is the conspicuously insubstantial rock on which aesthetic autonomy, as Shakespeare might have conceptualized it had he wished to do so, is founded.[22]

Shakespeare never underestimated the importance of what I have called the social agreement, a shared understanding that afforded the players some protection against interference. He made a lifelong habit of staying out of prison. The titles of several of his plays—*Much Ado about Nothing, As You Like It, Twelfth Night, or What You Will*—seem to reinforce Puck's genial claim to inconsequentiality. Ben Jonson claimed that his plays performed an important regulative function, but Shakespeare chose to imply that his art had no use-value whatever. It functioned only to give pleasure, or rather, to use the metaphoric image of Puck's epilogue, it existed as the audience's dream-work. If we observe that human beings in fact need pleasure and that a society's dream-work is vital, we could conclude that Shakespeare's triumphant cunning in *A Midsummer Night's Dream* is precisely to make his spectators forget that they are participating in a practical activity. His theater is powerful—and at least partially shielded from intervention—precisely because the audience believes that it is nonfunctional, nonuseful, and hence nonpractical.

And yet. It is striking that Shakespeare never actually returned to the claim that he had made at the end of *A Midsummer Night's Dream*. When in one of his last plays, *The Tempest*, he once again uses an epilogue to beg for the audience's pardon, it is in radically different terms that his character Prospero speaks:

> As you from crimes would pardoned be,
> Let your indulgence set me free. (Epilogue 19–20)

Here, as before, the epilogue form is used to break down the barrier between the world onstage and the world offstage, between performer and audience.²³ But where Puck had excused the play's limitations by comparing them to the bad dreams that members of the audience might have had, Prospero invokes the crimes that they might have committed. It is not the dreamlike meaninglessness of art that is the basis for its appeal to independence, or at least to protection, but something like the opposite: a strange insistence that its weaknesses, faults, and transgressions are secretly shared by those who sit in judgment upon them and who therefore stand equally in need of pardon.

How can we account for the distance between these two positions? The answer, I think, lies in Shakespeare's growing skepticism about the claim for autonomy that he had made, in the wake of Sidney, or rather a developing sense that the cost of this claim was too high. The extent of this cost is measured, perhaps, from the fact that the phrase "liberty to live after one's own law" could best serve as the motto for some of the most disturbing villains who haunted Shakespeare's imagination. These villains — Richard III, Edmund, Iago — share a desire for liberation, a murderous impatience with what Edmund calls "the plague of custom" and "the curiosity of nations." And they share as well a conviction that everyone in their world exists to be used for their own profit. The loathsome Oswald in *King Lear* gives voice to this conviction when he encounters the miserable, blinded Gloucester, who has been declared a traitor with a bounty on his head:

> A proclaimed prize! Most happy!
> That eyeless head of thine was first framed flesh
> To raise my fortunes. (4.5.222–24)

Oswald is disposed of easily — Gloucester's son Edgar beats him to death with a cudgel — but the sentiment he voices was not so readily dispatched. For it was, as Shakespeare well understood, a key principle not only of moral depravity but of playwriting. Gloucester, along with Oswald and all the other characters, were in fact created — "framed flesh" — in order to raise Shakespeare's fortunes. Shakespeare did not repudiate this fact—how could he, given his genius and his ambition? But the shift we see from "dream" to "crime" is a measure of his deepening awareness of the nature of his craft and the risks it entailed.

Notes

{ CHAPTER ONE }

1. Ben Jonson, *Timber, or Discoveries*. Cf. *Hamlet* 3.2.221 and *King John* 3.1.74.

2. All Shakespeare citations in this volume, unless otherwise noted, are from *The Norton Shakespeare,* ed. Stephen Greenblatt, Walter Cohen, Jean Howard, and Katharine Maus, 2nd. ed. (New York: W. W. Norton, 2008).

3. It is not only in erotic love that a refusal to acknowledge limits leads to disaster. Lear's absolutist claim to the love of his children—his assertion that he gave his daughters "everything" and his demand that they love him without measure—proves catastrophic. On the parental claim, see my "Lear's Anxiety," in *Learning to Curse: Essays in Early Modern Culture* (New York: Routledge, 1990).

4. *Aesthetic Theory*, ed. Gretel Adorno and Rolf Tiedemann, trans. Robert Hullot-Kentor (Minneapolis: University of Minnesota Press, 1997), 213.

5. Shakespeare was fascinated both by the ability of authority to hide vice and by the image of disease concealed beneath the smooth surface of the skin. The image saturates *Hamlet* in particular where the prince longs to probe a cancerous ulcer covered with tissue: "I'll tent him to the quick" (2.2.574). Here the special "medicine" of authority serves not to cure but to skin over the disease and therefore allow it to metastasize unseen.

{ CHAPTER TWO }

1. Beauty as defined by Alberti is a set of material features, but it bears a relation to the Neoplatonic "blossoming," or showing of internal perfection, articulated in the mid-fifteenth century by Marsilio Ficino: "The internal perfection produces the external. The former we can call goodness, the latter beauty. For this reason, we say that beauty is a certain blossom of goodness, by the charms of which blossom, as by a kind of bait, the hidden internal goodness attracts beholders. But since the cognition of our intellect takes its origin from the sense, we would never be aware of and never desire the goodness itself hidden in the heart of things if we were not attracted to it by the visible signs of external beauty." Ficino, quoted in *Renaissance Faces: Van Eyck to Titan* (London: National Gallery, 2008), 31.

2. See esp. Elizabeth Cropper, "On Beautiful Women, Parmigianino, *Petrarchismo*, and the Vernacular Style," *Art Bulletin* 58 (1976): 374–94, and Cropper, "The Beauty of Women: Problems in the Rhetoric of Renaissance Portraiture," in *Rewriting the Renaissance: The Discourse of Sexual Difference in Early Modern Europe*, ed. Margaret Ferguson, Maureen Quilligan, and Nancy Vickers (Chicago: University of Chicago Press, 1986), 175–90. On the representation of men in this tradition, see Stephen J. Campbell, "Eros in the Flesh: Petrarchan Desire, the Embodied Eros, and Male Beauty in Italian Art, 1500–1540," *Journal of Medieval and Early Modern Studies* 35 (2005): 629–62.

3. See Nancy Vickers, "The Body Re-Membered: Petrarchan Lyric and the Strategies of Description," in *Mimesis: From Mirror to Method, Augustine to Descartes*, ed. John D. Lyons and Stephen G. Nichols (Hanover, NH: University Press of New England, 1982), 100–109.

4. Schiller: "The content should do nothing, the form everything; for the wholeness of Man is affected by the form alone, and only individual powers by the content. However sublime and comprehensive it may be, the content always has a restrictive action upon the spirit, and only from the form is true aesthetic freedom to be expected. Therefore, the real artistic secret of the master consists in his *annihilating the material by means of the form*." *Aesthetic Education*, trans. Reginald Snell (New Haven: Yale University Press, 1954), 106.

Winckelmann: "[Its] forms are described by neither points nor lines, as such alone form beauty; consequently, a figure that belongs to neither this nor that particular person, nor expresses any condition of the spirit nor a sensation of passion, as such mix foreign aspects into beauty and disturb the unity. According to this concept [of *Unbezeichnung*] beauty should be like the most perfect water drawn from the lap of the spring, which, the less taste it has, the healthier it is considered to be, because it is purified of all foreign parts." Quoted in Simon Richter, *Laocoon's Body and the Aesthetics of Pain: Winckelmann, Lessing, Herder, Moritz, Goethe* (Detroit: Wayne State University Press, 1992), 15. Cf. Luca Giuiliani, "Winckelmanns Laokoon: Von der befristeten Eigenmächtigkeit des Kommentars," in G. W. Most, ed., *Commentaries. Kommentare* (Göttingen: Vandenhoeck & Ruprecht, 1999), 4:296–322, esp. 308.

5. Cf. Denis Donoghue, *Speaking of Beauty* (New Haven: Yale University Press, 2003).

6. Mark Frank, *LI sermons preached by the Reverend Dr. Mark Frank . . . being a course of sermons, beginning at Advent, and so continued through the festivals : to which is added a sermon preached at St. Pauls Cross, in the year forty-one, and then commanded to be printed by King Charles the First* (London: printed by Andrew Clark for John Martyn, Henry Brome, and Richard Chiswell, 1672), 89.

7. Ibid., 90–91. "The very natural inordination of our powers must needs give a kind of dull shadow to our exactest beauty, and silently speak the inward fault by some outward defect, though we are too dull, being of the same mold, to apprehend it; whilst there could be no such darkness in the face of Christ, no Genius in it which was not perfectly attractive, and exactly fitted to its place and office."

8. Ibid., 91.

9. John Wilkins, *An essay towards a real character, and a philosophical language* (London, 1668), chap. 8, pt. 5.

10. Thomas Aquinas, *Summa Theologica*, suppl. Q. 78. arts. 3, 5, 5:2876–77, and Q. 79, arts. 1–2, 5:2877–81, cited in Valentin Groebner, *Who Are You? Identification, Deception and Surveillance in Early Modern Europe* (Brooklyn, NY: Zone Books, 2007), 8.

11. Frank, *LI sermons*, 91.

12. British Library, Additional MS 23,069, fol. 11, cited in Laura Lunger Knoppers, *Constructing Cromwell: Ceremony, Portrait and Print, 1645–1661* (New York: Cambridge University Press, 2000), 80.

13. Bassanio continues in the same vein, intensifying the sense of grotesquery:

> So are those crispèd, snaky, golden locks
> Which makes such wanton gambols with the wind
> Upon supposèd fairness, often known
> To be the dowry of a second head,
> The skull that bred them in the sepulchre. (3.2.92–96)

Some at least of the anxiety in Bassanio's celebration of Portia's beauty, in her picture, is linked to a current of fear that beauty and chastity are opposed to one another. See Pietro Aretino's sonnet on Titian's 1537–38 portrait of Eleonora Gonzago, Duchess of Urbino: "The union of colours laid in by Titian's brush expresses, besides the concord that reigns in Eleonora, her gentle spirit. Modesty [*modestia*] is seated with her in an attitude of humility, purity resides in her dress, modesty [*vergogna*] veils and honours her breast and hair. Love fixes on her his lordly glance. Chastity and beauty, eternal enemies, are in her likeness and between her eyelashes the throne of the Graces is seen" (*Renaissance Faces*, 30). The portrait has just that blankness of expression that I have tried to analyze.

14. Lucretius, *On the Nature of Things*, trans. Martin Ferguson Smith (Indianapolis: Hackett, 2001), 4:1152–54.

15. Ibid., 4:1160–64.

16. Ibid., 4:1176–77, 1181–85.

17. See the brilliant reflections on this phenomenon in Joel Fineman's *Shakespeare's Perjured Eye: The Invention of Poetic Subjectivities in the Sonnets* (Berkeley: University of California Press, 1986), esp. 291.

18. Neville Williams, *Power and Paint: A History of the Englishwoman's Toilet* (London: Longmans, 1957), 18–20, 37–38.

19. *Works of J. Lyly*, ed. J. W. Bond (Oxford: Oxford University Press, 1902), 1:184, 21–23. Venus's mole and Helen's scar are endlessly repeated

motifs in the late sixteenth and early seventeenth centuries. See, for example, Thomas Dekker, *The Gull's Hornbook* (1600), chap. 1: "How wonderfully is the world altered! And no marvel, for it has lien sick almost five thousand years; so that it is no more like the old *théâtre du monde,* than old Paris Garden is like the king's Garden at Paris.

"What an excellent workman therefore were he, that could cast the Globe of it into a new mould: and not to make it look like Mullineux his globe, with a round face sleeked and washed over with whites of eggs; but to have it *in plano,* as it was at first, with all the ancient circles, lines, parallels, and figures; representing indeed all the wrinkles, cracks, crevices, and flaws that (like the mole on Helen's cheek, being *cos amoris,*) stuck upon it at the first creation and made it look most lovely: but now those furrows are filled up with ceruse and vermilion; yet all will not do, it appears more ugly. Come, come; it would be but a bald world, but that it wears a periwig; the body of it is foul, like a birding-piece, by being too much heated; the breath of it stinks like the mouths of chambermaids by feeding on so many sweetmeats: and, though to purge it will be a sorer labour than the cleansing of Augeas' stable, or the scouring of Moorditch, yet *Ille ego qui quondam*; I am the Pasquil's madcap that will do't."

20. In the fantasy of a seventeenth-century French poet, beauty marks originated when Cupid trapped a fly that had alighted on his mother's breast and held it there

> so all can see
> How suddenly the breast seems quite
> A dazzling, bright, effulgent white,
> As 'round a cloud of blackish hue
> The sky becomes a brighter blue.

(Quoted—without identification—in Richard Corson, *Fashions in Makeup from Ancient to Modern Times* [London: Peter Owen, 1972], 166.) In the *Divine Weeks,* Du Bartas asks God to grant that

> the greatest spot you spie

In all my Frame, may be but as the Fly,
Which on her Ruff (whiter than whitest snowes)
To whiten white, the fairest Virgin sowes:
(Or like the Velvet on her brow: or, like
The dunker Mole on Venus dainty Cheek:)
And, that a few faults may but lustre bring
To my high furies where I sweetest sing.

(Trans. Josuah Sylvester, 2nd book of the 4th day of the 2nd week, 553.)

21. "The word 'stain' first enters the play when Iachimo describes the mole to Posthumus: 'You do remember / This stain upon her?' At that point, Posthumus, who is already convinced of Innogen's infidelity through the manacle, replies, 'Ay, and it doth confirm / Another stain as big as hell can hold' (2.4.138–40). The mole is used to evoke the stain of womankind associated with Eve and original sin in the second wager scene. Yet when Iachimo first sees the mole in Innogen, he describes it as 'cinque-spotted, like the crimson drops / I'th' bottom of a cowslip' (2.2.38–39): its red spots are delicately patterned like the inside of a flower. The flower image associated with the mole becomes a stain when Iachimo sullies it to entrap Posthumus, and those associations of the erotic body and sexual guilt migrate to the bloody cloth." Valerie Wayne, "The Women's Parts of *Cymbeline*," in Jonathan Gil Harris and Natasha Korda, eds., *Staged Properties in Early Modern English Drama* (Cambridge: Cambridge University Press, 2002), 298. I am indebted to Valerie Wayne for valuable suggestions.

{ CHAPTER THREE }

1. Carl Schmitt, *The Concept of the Political*, trans. George Schwab (Chicago: University of Chicago Press, 1996), 37.

2. For the argument that Shylock has been granted the boon of citizenship, see Julia Reinhard Lupton, *Citizen-Saints: Shakespeare and Political Theology* (Chicago: University of Chicago Press, 2005), 100.

3. Louise Richardson, *What Terrorists Want* (New York: Random House, 2006), 104–35. See Navid Kermani, *Dynamit des Geistes: Mar-*

tyrium, Islam und Nihilismus (Göttingen: Wallstein, 2002).

4. See http://www.stsimonoftrent.com for a modern rehearsal of anti-Judaism in its traditional vicious form.

5. "The Jewish Holiday of Purim, by Dr. Umayma Ahmad Al-Jalahma of King Faysal University in Al-Dammam," *Al-Riyadh*, March 10, 2002. (Source: Middle East Media Research Institute.) In the wake of protests, there was some criticism of Ms. Al-Jalahma's article within the Saudi media. Othman Mahmud al-Sini, a columnist for *al-Watan,* conceded that "the Jewish dependence on blood dates centuries back, and became notorious through Shakespeare's *Merchant of Venice.* In this play, the Jewish merchant Shylock demanded to slice a pound of flesh from the play's main character, in exchange for a debt owed to him." But, he noted, "this is not the right time for raising this issue" (April 1, 2002).

6. This initiative—the independent, entrepreneurial decision to devise a cunning plot—serves, along with Shylock's savage wit and perhaps his obsession with money, to give Shakespeare a basis for identifying personally with his character.

7. Shylock's claim could be disputed: one could say that Antonio spits on him not as a Jew but as a moneylender. After all, earlier in the play, when Shylock offers to lend money without taking interest, Antonio accepts with unwontedly gracious words: "Hie thee, gentle Jew." To reinforce the pun on "gentle," he adds to Bassanio: "The Hebrew will turn Christian; he grows kind" (1.3.173–74). But, of course, for a Jew whose livelihood is restricted to and depends on usury, Antonio's epithet "gentle" is another form of spitting.

8. On this equation in the visual arts, see Ruth Mellinkoff, *Outcasts: Signs of Otherness in Northern European Art of the Late Middle Ages* (Berkeley: University of California Press, 1993); Deborah Strickland, *Saracens, Demons, Jews: Making Monsters in Medieval Art* (Princeton: Princeton University Press, 2003); and Joshua Trachtenberg, *The Devil and the Jews* (New York: Harper and Row, 1966).

9. "The Shylock we have been following in the play," writes Derek Cohen in an impassioned essay on *The Merchant of Venice* ("The Question of Shylock," in *The Politics of Shakespeare* [Houndsmills, Baisingstoke: St. Martin's Press, 1993]), "was born or created for just this mo-

ment—to raise his knife and thrust Antonio in the heart. . . . He and we
have been primed for a *killing* by every word he has spoken and that has
been spoken about him in the play" (32). Shylock's collapse, in Cohen's
view, is "a dramatic outrage committed on the audience" (31) as well as
on the character.

10. *Othello* begins where *The Merchant of Venice* ends—with an alien
who has converted and been assimilated, but who is treated anyway, at
least in some quarters, as an outsider.

11. Kenneth Gross, *Shylock* Is *Shakespeare* (Chicago: University of
Chicago Press, 2006).

12. It is this force, as well as Othello's flair for theatrical self-display,
that is reflected in his acceptance of the Venetian senate's charge to
command the garrison at Cyprus:

> I do agnize
> A natural and prompt alacrity
> I find in hardness, and do undertake
> This present wars against the Ottomites. (1.3.229–32)

13. *Othello* 5.2.356. A famous textual crux: the reading in the folio
text is "Judean," but in the quarto text it is "Indian." Both readings are
entirely possible. In the former case the emphasis is on the hatred felt
by and toward the "circumcisèd dog" (5.3.364); in the latter it is on what
Europeans presumed to be the ignorance of easily duped natives. Hence
"Judean" seems closer conceptually to "a malignant and a turbaned
Turk" (5.2.362) whom the suicidal Othello recalls, while "Indian" seems
closer to Othello's account of himself as one "that loved not wisely but
too well" (5.3.353).

14. In a fourteenth-century copy of John of Foxton's *Book of Cosmog-
raphy* (Trinity College Library, Cambridge, MS R.15.21.fol. 14v), Melan-
cholia is depicted as a black Ethiopian stabbing himself (cf. Strickland,
Saracens, Demons, Jews, 35, 84, and fig. 2). A mid-fifteenth-century Ba-
varian *Antichrist* (Staatsbibliothek zu Berlin, Preussischer Kulturbesitz,
Berlin, MA germ. F. 733, fol. 4), also in Strickland (plate 7), shows an
Ethiopian, a Saracen, and a Jew adoring Antichrist. The upper register

of the folio conjoins a group of hooded Ethiopians with three Blem-myai—men "whose heads / Do grow beneath their shoulders," as Othel-lo defines them (1.3.143–44). "Described independently of each other as thoroughly wicked," Strickland writes, it "makes a certain amount of logical medieval sense that Jews, Muslim, Ethiopians, and Monstrous Races would all meet in the service of Antichrist" (228).

{ CHAPTER FOUR }

1. Thomas Starkey, *A Dialogue between Pole and Lupset*, ed. T. F. Mayer (London: Office of the Royal Historical Society, University College, London, 1989), 104.

2. Bernard Williams, *Shame and Necessity* (Berkeley: University of California Press, 1993), 42.

3. Ibid., 94.

4. The line I have quoted—and much of the scene from which it is taken—appears in the quarto version of the play published in 1607–8 and is omitted from the folio version (1628).

5. Officially sanctioned torture in England was at its height during the reigns of Elizabeth and James. "In the highest cases of treasons," Bacon wrote in a memorandum for King James, "torture is used for dis-covery and not for evidence." Elizabeth Hanson, "Torture and Truth in Renaissance England," *Representations* 34 (1991): 53–84; John H. Lang-bein, *Torture and the Law of Proof: Europe and England in the Ancien Régime* (Chicago: University of Chicago Press, 1977), 90. Shakespeare seems to take this acceptance for granted at the close of *Othello* when Iago re-fuses to explain why he has devised his fiendish plot:

Demand me nothing. What you know, you know.
From this time forth I never will speak word. (5.2.309–10)

One of the bystanders is morally outraged—"What, not to pray?"—but another has a response at least as characteristic of Jacobean Eng-land: "Torments will ope your lips" (5.2.311–12).

To authorize torture, official Council warrants first had to be ob-tained, which specified the names of the victims and listed their alleged offences. "But the reign of Elizabeth was the period when torture was most used in England. Of the eighty-one documented cases between 1540 and 1640, fifty-three (65 per cent) were Elizabethan. Before 1589 torture was undertaken at the Tower, and between 1589 and 1603 at Bridewell in London, where special equipment was available." John Guy, *Tudor England* (Oxford: Oxford University Press, 1988), 318. According to Langbein, "We suggest that the power to torture did inhere in the prerogative, not affirmatively but defensively. It derived from the doctrine of sovereign immunity. The sovereign was immune from suit in his own courts. Not only were the King and Council immune, they could immunize their agents" (*Torture*, 130).

6. Quoted in Langbein, *Torture*, 82–83.

7. Perhaps Cornwall is thinking about how he will justify torturing an aristocrat, something that was against English practice. Gloucester, however, is not at all Cornwall's equal.

{ CHAPTER FIVE }

1. Adorno repeatedly affirms aesthetic autonomy only to qualify the assertion or to withdraw it altogether. "Even the most sublime artwork takes up a determinate attitude to empirical reality by stepping outside of the constraining spell it casts, not once and for all, but rather ever and again, concretely, unconsciously polemical toward this spell at each historical moment. . . . Art's double character as both autonomous and *fait social* is incessantly reproduced on the level of its autonomy. It is by virtue of this relation to the empirical that artworks recuperate, neutralized, what once was literally and directly experienced in life and what was expelled by spirit. Artworks participate in enlightenment because they do not lie" (*Aesthetic Theory*, 5).

2. *The Encyclopaedia of Architecture: Historical, Theoretical, and Practical* (New York: Crown Publishers, 1982), 795.

3. "Then the mutiny of the people encreasing, they went to the Bishops house, willing him to goe about the matter, that they might haue either bread or peace: whereupon some of the counselers of the Pseudosenat, pittying their owne, and the misery of the people, with the Bishop of Lions, the Duke of Nemours, and others of the chiefest of

the rebellion entred in counsell, whether they ought to admit the King vpon reasonable conditions, specially hauing their autonomy." Antony Colynet, *The true history of the ciuill vvarres of France, betweene the French King Henry the 4. and the Leaguers. Gathered from the yere of our Lord 1585. vntill this present October. 1591* (London, 1591), 8:840. "Autonomy" here refers to the ability of the city to maintain its civic independence, but Colynet brings out a contradiction in it. Those who propose a negotiation with the king hope to maintain "their autonomy." But the Duke of Nemours sees that autonomy as lost, precisely in such a negotiation: "The matter being discoursed, and some altogether inclining to peace, withstanding that counsell, the Duke of Nemours, gouernour of the city, said in great anger, that he had rather see the City consumed then lost: meaning that if it were yéelded vnto the King, he estéemed it lost, and going foorth in great anger, would not be present any longer in such deliberation." For the duke, there is no such thing as submitting to the king—admitting him to the city—and retaining the city's autonomy. After his angry departure, his position, however, does not prevail: "Notwithstanding, they agréed all to send Ambassadors to the King, to entreate of an vniuersall peace."

4. London, 1623. The definition sits in a peculiar anticipatory relation to Kant's conception of "moral liberty"—the law of an autonomous will—but it is beyond the scope of this book, and of my own abilities, to follow the complex twisting path that leads from one to the other.

5. *Mr. William Shakespeares comedies, histories, & tragedies* (London, 1623).

6. Anthony James West, *The Shakespeare First Folio: The History of the Book,* 2 vols. (Oxford: Oxford University Press, 2001), 1:3. A few plays might, Bodley acknowledged, be worth keeping, but "the more I think upon it, the more it doth distaste me that such kind of books should be vouchsafed a room, in so noble a library."

7. *The Trew Law of Free Monarchies: or the Reciprock and Mutuall Duetie Betwixt a Free King, and his Naturall Subiects,* in *King James VI and I, Political Writings,* ed. Johann P. Sommerville (Cambridge: Cambridge University Press, 1994), 73, 75.

8. Cited in Debora Shuger, *Censorship and Cultural Sensibility: The*

Regulation of Language in Tudor-Stuart England (Philadelphia: University of Pennsylvania Press, 2006), 3.

9. Cited in Ernst H. Kantorowicz, *The King's Two Bodies: A Study in Mediaeval Political Theology* (Princeton: Princeton University Press, 1957), 99.

10. Cf. Oliver Arnold, "The King of Comedy: The Role of the Ruler and the Rule of Law in Shakespeare's Comedies," *Genre* 31 (1968): 1–31.

11. Ernst H. Kantorowicz, *The King's Two Bodies: A Study in Mediaeval Political Theology* (Princeton: Princeton University Press, 1957), 26.

12. Ibid., 390.

13. Ibid., 423, summarizing Coke's remarks in *Calvin's Case*: ". . . one a natural body . . ., and this body is of the creation of Almighty God, and is subject to death . . . and the other is a politic body. . . framed by the policy of man . . . and in this capacity the King is esteemed to be immortal, invisible, not subject to death."

14. See my *Renaissance Self-Fashioning: From More to Shakespeare* (Chicago: University of Chicago Press, 1980), chap. 5. The most apposite figure of absolute autonomy in Marlowe is Tamburlaine.

15. *Sir Philip Sidney's "An Apology for Poetry,"* ed. Geoffrey Shepherd (London: Thomas Nelson and Sons, 1965), 99–100. All Sidney citations are from this source unless otherwise noted.

16. See the discussion of this exception in Jeffrey Knapp, "Spenser the Priest," *Representations* 81 (2003): 61–78.

17. Lucretius, *On the Nature of Things*, trans. Martin Ferguson Smith (Indianapolis: Hackett, 2001), 2:700–708.

18. Sidney's "Apology for Poetry," 102.

19. Ibid., 101

20. There is a glimpse at least of aristocratic politics when, glancing back at *A Midsummer Night's Dream*, Shakespeare plays brilliantly in *Antony and Cleopatra* with this idea of an escape from nature. "You laugh when boys or women tell their dreams; / Is't not your trick?" Cleopatra asks her Roman captor Dolabella, and then launches into her extravagant dream of the Emperor Antony:

His legs bestrid the ocean; his reared arm

Crested the world. His voice was propertied
As all the tunèd spheres, and that to friends;
But when he meant to quail and shake the orb,
He was as rattling thunder. For his bounty,
There was no winter in't; an autumn 'twas,
That grew the more by reaping. His delights
Were dolphin-like; they showed his back above
The element they lived in. In his livery
Walked crowns and crownets. Realms and islands were
As plates dropped from his pocket. (5.2.73–74, 81–91)

When Dolabella tries to awaken her from her reverie—"Cleopatra!"
—Cleopatra asks him whether he thinks "there was, or might be, such
a man / As this I dreamt of?" To his polite but firm no, she replies passionately:

You lie, up to the hearing of the gods.
But if there be, or ever were one such,
It's past the size of dreaming. Nature wants stuff
To vie strange forms with fancy; yet, t'imagine
An Antony were nature's piece 'gainst fancy,
Condemning shadows quite. (5.2.91–99)

"Nature wants stuff / To vie strange forms with fancy": we are back
to the center of Sidney's argument that in the competition between
imagination and nature, the liberated imagination must invariably win,
precisely because it alone is capable of creating "strange forms." But
Cleopatra turns the argument on its head: the reality of Antony is "past
the size of dreaming" and hence his existence is nature's triumphant
counterstroke, proving the inferiority of mere "shadows."

The claim, however, is hedged about with qualifications and ironies,
and not only because the audience has seen Antony, in his all-too-human limitations as well as his powers, for itself. Cleopatra's own words
convey doubts, even as she makes her claims, or rather those claims are
themselves marked as the product of fancy: "t'imagine / An Antony."

It will be because she prefers this fancy to the miserable reality of her captivity that Cleopatra will kill herself:

> methinks I hear
> Antony call. I see him rouse himself
> To praise my noble act. I hear him mock
> The luck of Caesar, which the gods give men
> To excuse their after wrath. Husband, I come. (5.2.274–78)

21. See Jane Clare, *"Art Made Tongue-Tied by Authority": Elizabethan and Jacobean Dramatic Censorship* (Manchester: Manchester University Press, 1990); Richard Dutton, *Mastering the Revels: The Regulation and Censorship of English Renaissance Drama* (London: Macmillan, 1991); Annabel Patterson, *Censorship and Interpretation: The Conditions of Writing and Reading in Early Modern England* (Madison: University of Wisconsin Press, 1984).

22. This latent conceptualization is not entirely alien to Adorno's own theory of aesthetic autonomy, autonomy dependent upon the embrace of purposelessness. For Adorno the most ambitious modernist artworks emphasize "through their powerlessness and superfluity in the empirical world . . . the element of powerlessness in their own content" (*Aesthetic Theory*, 104). By emphasizing this powerlessness, art challenges a bourgeois social order obsessed with the accumulation of power and exchange value. But these formulations depend for their full meaning on the Kantian formulation of art's "purposefulness without purpose," a formulation that lies beyond the horizon of Shakespeare's own artistic (and commercial) enterprise. Cf. Sianne Ngai, "The Cuteness of the Avant-Garde," *Critical Inquiry* 31 (2005): 811–47. There is an intriguing relation between "cuteness" as analyzed by Ngai in kewpie dolls, Japanese kitsch, and the like and Shakespeare's diminutive fairies. A discussion of this relation would begin with the observation that Shakespeare precisely made the fairies—definitively, thanks to his influence—diminutive. On deliberate inconsequentiality, see Paul Yachnin, *Stage-Wrights: Shakespeare, Jonson, Middleton, and the Making of Theatrical Value* (Philadelphia: University of Pennsylvania Press, 1997). There are

important theoretical reflections on the claim to inconsequentiality in Pierre Bourdieu, *Outline of a Theory of Practice*, trans. Richard Nice (Cambridge: Cambridge University Press, 1977).

23. "Please you, draw near," Prospero says (5.1.322), just before he speaks the epilogue. The line is often represented as an address to the other characters, whom he is inviting to enter his cell, but the injunction to "draw near" seems even more fitting as an address to the audience. It is as if Prospero expects that they will all come closer or lean forward.

Index